D0713507

THE
POWER
TO
LEAD

THE
POWER
TO
LEAD

Lessons in Creating
Your Unique Masterpiece

Gregg Thompson
Bruna Martinuzzi

SelectBooks, Inc.
New York

The Power to Lead
Lessons in Creating Your Unique Masterpiece

Copyright © 2009 by Gregg Thompson and Bruna Martinuzzi

All rights reserved. Published in the United States of America. No part of this book may be reproduced or transmitted in any form or by any means, graphic, electronic, or mechanical, including photocopying, recording, taping or by any information storage or retrieval system, without the permission in writing from the publisher.

This edition published by SelectBooks, Inc.
For information address SelectBooks, Inc., New York, New York.

First Edition

ISBN 978-1-59079-191-2

Library of Congress Cataloging-in-Publication Data

Thompson, Gregg, 1950-

The power to lead : lessons in creating your unique masterpiece / Gregg Thompson, Bruna Martinuzzi. -- 1st ed.

p. cm.

Includes bibliographical references and index.

ISBN 978-1-59079-191-2 (hardbound : alk. paper)

1. Leadership. 2. Executive ability. I. Martinuzzi, Bruna, 1947– II. Title.

HD57.7.T4673 2008

658.4'092--dc22

2008047282

Manufactured in the United States of America

10 9 8 7 6 5 4 3 2 1

To Judy, for choosing to fill her life's masterpiece
with service and sacrifice.

GREGG THOMPSON

To Saul, who taught me to caress the rainbow.

BRUNA MARTINUZZI

The great thing in this world is not so much where we are,
but in what direction we are moving.

OLIVER WENDELL HOLMES JR., AMERICAN JURIST

CONTENTS

ACKNOWLEDGMENTS

We are life-long students of leadership. Some of our greatest teachers have been our clients—leaders with exceptional passion, energy, vision, and insight. Special thanks go to Thomas W. Steipp, Brian Traquair, Marsha Royer, Karin Kirkpatrick, Mike Szczechura, Scott Duncan, Jeffrey C. Hawkins, Mark Ahrens-Townsend, John Sage, and Willard (Dub) Hay for helping us to paint pictures of personal and professional excellence—leadership that cultivates the very best in people and organizations. Grateful acknowledgment is given to Mady Gorrell for her work in managing the production and publication of this book. Special thanks go to Joan Peterson and Debbie Rand, for their tireless efforts in proofreading many versions of the manuscript.

We are also ever grateful to the Bluepoint Leadership Development community members who have committed their lives to helping leaders everywhere create personal masterpieces.

INTRODUCTION

This is a different book on leadership. It does not advance a particular model or philosophy about leadership, nor does it chronicle the exploits of the great political leaders like Mahatma Gandhi or Winston Churchill, or the commercial feats of business giants like Bill Gates and Jack Welch. This book is simply about you, your leadership ambitions, and how you can prepare yourself for this important calling. Yes, we do mean *calling*. Leadership is at the core of all important human endeavors, whether commercial or social, political or humanitarian, scientific or artistic. And it is a role that should not be stepped into lightly. People will count on you. Organizations will put their very existence in your hands. You will affect people's careers and have an impact on their lives and families. Leadership is that important.

Am I capable? Can I make a difference? These are the questions we all ask ourselves when confronted with the daunting challenge of leadership. The good news is that we are indeed capable, and we can make a difference. Humans are naturally wired to lead. We are drawn to community, whether corporate, social, or family. We seek a tomorrow that is better than today. We see our lives as journeys on roads shared with others. Joining others in the pursuit of a better tomorrow is at the heart of the human experience ... and we are all naturally gifted to do this work. Unfortunately, many of us use only a very small portion of our leadership capability, choosing instead to covet the lives of those courageous men and women who step to the front of the line with little more than ambition in their eyes, fear in their hearts, and a blurry roadmap in their hands. These are the all too-rare individuals who have discovered that the real power to lead comes from within, and is theirs to seize.

1

This book describes the inner journey of leadership. Its singular goal is to help you find the power to lead within yourself–those natural motivations and capabilities that, paradoxically, both set you apart from others and draw you to them. In the 25 years that we have been training and coaching some of the finest leaders, we have learned one important thing … true development of the leader occurs at the deepest personal levels and manifests itself in a significant increase in personal power. This is not power over others, but rather the power to inspire, engage, and serve others. This is the power to make a real difference in a team, an organization, and even the world.

In this book, we use the enduring art of oil painting as a metaphor for leadership. When we view a great painting, we may be tempted to see it as the product of a linear, orderly process, moving from inspiration to framing. This is rarely the case. Painting is a much more complex endeavor. To create a masterpiece, the artist needs to prepare the canvas well, assemble oils with just the right pigments, and move the oils about on the canvas until that moment when a complete painting is formed. Leadership is a similar dynamic process.

Just as an artist begins a great painting with a well-primed surface, in *Part One* of the book, **Your Canvas**, we will help you explore how you can prepare your own leadership canvas. The artist creates a solid frame: The material is stretched taut, all waste is trimmed and a primer prepares the surface. The bigger and the better a canvas is, the greater the potential for a wonderful work of art. The slings and arrows of organizational life will provide ample opportunities to paint a masterpiece rich in experiences. This part of the book will help clarify your thinking as you prepare to lead. What are your most important values and aspirations? How can your passions fuel your leadership? How does your personality lend itself to influencing others?

Great artists are known to fill their palettes with a wide array of pigments so that they can readily create the perfect color that captures the often indescribable image that is in their minds. In *Part Two* of the book, **Your Palette**, we will challenge you to fully explore all of your unique talents, emotions, and personal traits–and include these in your unique leadership palette.

Oil paint remains wet longer than many other types of artists' materials, enabling the artist to change the color, texture, or form of the image at any time. Rarely does the artist leave the paint exactly as first applied. The masterpiece is created by moving the paint already on the canvas, blending it with other colors, changing the texture. Art conservators do not consider an oil painting completely dry for many years. So it is with leadership. In *Part Three,* **Your Masterpiece**, you will be encouraged to see your leadership development as a dynamic process lasting for your entire career.

Whether you are an emerging leader about to take on your first managerial role, a mid-level leader wanting to accelerate your readiness for a more senior role, or a seasoned executive looking to lift your leadership game for one more major career push, *The Power to Lead* is written for you. In some respects, you will find this book to be a primer for leadership; in other respects, you will find in its pages, the most complex and challenging aspects of this important human endeavor. The best pages, however, are those you will write as you complete your personal leadership explorations at the end of each chapter. The book invites you to take a thoughtful and candid look at yourself before setting out to lead others.

We hope this book will be your guide on this most important journey, your leadership journey. We wish you well.

PART ONE

Your Canvas

CHAPTER ONE

A Fire Within

The Power of Motivation

"I want to make a dent in the universe."

Steve Jobs

The desire to lead is an essential requirement for being a good leader. Leadership is a rewarding, yet often a difficult and arduous journey. Without a burning desire to lead, that journey can be devoid of pleasure. Great leaders possess not only the will to lead, they also have no doubt about their motives. They are clear about why they chose to lead.

What motivates you to lead? Leaders are driven by varied aspirations ranging from accumulating wealth to saving the planet. While many of these motivators will adequately fuel leadership for a time, the great leaders who make a significant and sustained impact on their organizations are usually compelled by high level motivations that will positively impact many people. They set out to change, for the better, their corner of the world. At the same time, they know that thinking big leads to expansive actions, while thinking small inevitably leads to limited outcomes. So they derive their inspiration, not from bite-size goals, but from having big, audacious goals—a fierce, inward commitment to making a difference.

7

This is the oil that fires their internal furnace–it's what fuels their power to create. It's easy to spot these leaders. There is an energy that radiates when they speak about their desire to achieve these higher goals. This desire is at the heart of their leadership behavior, characterized by a certain *noblesse oblige,* which confers, that with power and prestige comes social responsibility. Translated for leaders, it means that those who are graced with positions of leadership–with special talents or gifts–have an obligation to make the best use of these gifts. They are bound to do their very best for the collective good.

Having the desire to lead, and the will to embark on this journey, gives leaders the fortitude to stay the course no matter what comes their way. So how does one increase one's motivation to lead even in the face of the chaos and uncertainty that characterize our times? To borrow Stephen Covey's famous words: "Imagine how you want to be remembered as a leader." What legacy do you want to leave behind? What have you done so far to accomplish this vision of yourself? Are you pleased with how the vision is unfolding?

Think back to a time when your motivation to lead was at its apex; what was it that made the difference? Can you tap into this past vision to your advantage? How can you play a direct part in changing your corner of the world for the better? This is your very own leadership vessel: are you steering the ship or are the winds taking you wherever they blow? Do unexpected derailments cause you to cut off the engines and stop sailing, wasting the precious time you have as a leader? What steps can you take today to chart the way for your ship to travel to the destination you intend? What big, audacious goals can you set? How can you make this journey truly yours?

We increase our motivation to lead by immersing ourselves in actions and endeavors that constantly challenge us to expand our talents by developing and maintaining a passionate curiosity–being an ageless learner–and by cultivating an ardent interest in shaping and steering the future. Successful leaders are builders, not maintainers. What do you want to build? Where do you want to go from where you are right now?

The motivation to lead is a daily practice. To ensure that your vision of yourself as a leader becomes a defining component of who you are, consider making the vision a part of your daily thoughts so that it becomes firmly embedded in your subconscious mind and then allow it to play for you. Our subconscious mind has a powerful influence on what we consciously perceive and the decisions we make. It influences our behavior because the subconscious mind makes our outside world reflect the vision that we have stored internally. We encourage you to power up by painting a brilliant internal vision of yourself, and then anchoring it into your subconscious. This is a superb mental state to be in.

But perhaps the biggest boost to increasing your motivation to lead is recognizing that leadership is a state of mind: it's about your belief in yourself as a leader, in trusting that you will be able to handle whatever comes your way, no matter how unplanned or unexpected. It's being aware of your limitations and going beyond them anyway. It's accepting the natural self-doubt that is the invisible companion of every leader who is attempting to accomplish great things, and it's about not letting that self-doubt inhibit your leadership, but instead taking charge and grabbing the power—the power to accomplish what you set out to do. Dare to believe that something inside you is infinitely greater than the events of the day. We encourage you to break through the upper bounds that you may have mentally set up for yourself.

Just as it is important to increase one's motivation, it is equally important to be vigilant about not losing motivation along the way, which can easily happen given the challenges that leaders face. Great leaders ensure that they stay motivated by having a crystal clear idea of their purpose in life, of what really matters to them. This provides the context for everything that they do. They don't lose sight of what gives their life its deeper meaning, of what it's all for. They carve out time in their busy lives to think about what's important to them. They ensure that they lead significant lives. They have a fine-grained awareness of their values and they periodically re-examine those values to evaluate whether they still reflect who they are and what they want. But more than just values, it is passion that gives their life direction. To them, passion is values on steroids.

Leadership is most certainly a bumpy and solitary trail: It's not for the faint-hearted. As Ron Crossland and Boyd Clarke said: "Some will judge you unfairly, blaming you for their lack of success. Others will expect resources you cannot give, answers that you do not have, and permission you cannot grant. You will be misquoted. Your judgment will be questioned. You will certainly stumble. Failure will stalk you like a predator."[1] Along the way you will receive a lot of feedback, both good and bad. The few moments of gratitude, the long hours and the personal sacrifices that come with the job often result in a loss of motivation to lead. As a leader, you need to reconnect with your passion, to rediscover the mental energy you felt when you first set out on your leadership adventure.

What gives your life its significance? Do you have a passion that gets you to jump out of bed in the morning, raring to go? Are you motivated by just breaking even, ensuring that you live your emotional and spiritual life with neither profit nor loss? Is your life filled with blind alleys? What can you do to shine a light on your path? Think back to the infinite possibilities of playtime when you were a child. What can you do to bring play into your ordered, daily life? What risks can you take to live passionately every day? Do you stay within the lines when you use your crayons? What would happen if you decide to sweep your crayons right across the page?

Remember when you were a child and you arbitrarily used any color to create your daily masterpiece? What can you do to stretch your imagination to paint your portrait as a leader, without being restrained by the erroneous notion that there exists a correct set of colors–letting your imagination flow over all the possibilities of greatness that are in you? If you are at an impasse in your leadership and have lost some of the passion, what can you do to renew yourself, to recover that initial spark, to reconnect with your initial passion and rekindle that spirit?

Studying the lives of great leaders in history can add to our motivation to lead. If they can do it, why can't you? Inspiration is gained from individuals like Nelson Mandela, Winston Churchill, and Martin Luther King; entertainers like Oprah Winfrey, Charlie Chaplin, and Lucille Ball; poets like Dylan Thomas and T. S. Elliot; thinkers like Albert Einstein and John Maynard Keynes; icons like Mother Teresa, Princess Diana, Muhammad Ali, and Charles Lindbergh. Absorb lessons from these giants and become infused with the inspiration that motivated them. Read about the struggles and victories of these leaders, and increase your conviction to succeed in your own leadership quest. Consider studying other leaders as additional sources of inspiration for your own leadership motivation.

We also encourage you to think about your wants, these strong desires or inclinations. They are also sometimes referred to as preferences. Thomas Khun, the philosopher who coined the expression 'paradigm shift' said: "Power is the ability to satisfy one's wants through the control of preferences and/or opportunities."

- What impact do these desires or inclinations have on your leadership?
- What particular preferences might be influencing these wants?
- What can you do to reframe these preferences?
- Are there any circumstances or opportunities that you can control or alter to make it more favorable to have these desires satisfied?
- How much psychological energy are you devoting to pursuing your wants?
- Are these desires causing you to ignore certain relevant information, ideas, or feelings?
- What are the gaps between what you have and what you could have? What is this motivating you to do? What can you do to bridge that gap?

In addition to being aware of their manifestation and impact, we also need to be aware of the path these desires or wants can take, shifting from being a low intensity motivator to a high intensity one. Consider this scenario: your organization experiences you as a leader who is strongly motivated by stability and security. Deep down, you also have a desire for continued personal growth and self-realization. You wake up one morning, having fulfilled all the key performance indicators for your position and asking yourself the proverbial question: "Is that all there is?" You now find that your desire for personal growth and self-realization which were perched on the edges, are shifting to the middle and becoming an all consuming need. This impacts your behavior, causing you to promote risk taking. Unlike you, your organization may not have changed and your need may now not be in line with your organization's strategic imperatives. Organizations seek consistency and the unpredictability of your behavior will surely erode your authenticity and diminish your power as a leader in the eyes of your constituents. Being aware of the shift and its impact is powerful information for you in your leadership. It will guide you to better decisions and guard you from being blind-sided. Your needs and wants, then, are important elements of your palette.

This takes us to your values–those principles, standards or qualities that we consider most worthwhile. In painting parlance, value–the relative lightness or darkness of a color–is the strongest element dominating our visual experience. Without good value structure, the painting appears flat and uninteresting. The same can be said of our own value system. Just as values are the strongest element in a painting, so values dominate our ethos. They are a prism through which we see the world. They fashion our sense of identity. As with needs and wants, values mold us and color our behaviors and actions. They provide the yardstick that we use to differentiate what is right and wrong, good and bad, desirable and undesirable. Most often, our values were developed early on in our life and are, therefore, not easily changed. They stem from experiences we have had with people that we admire and value, people who are important to us, like parents, teachers, mentors or coaches. We are emotionally invested in our values.

Understanding what we value, then, is another dimension for discovering what prompts our behaviors and actions. There is something very compelling and powerful when a leader is very clear about his or her values and lives these unequivocally every day.

- What are the values that are most important to you? What do you stand for?
- Are your goals and objectives in sync with your values?
- Do you live your values visibly every day? Would those who know you be able to easily articulate what you stand for? Have your choices been consistent with your values?
- Which values do you aspire to and want more of?
- What are you willing to sacrifice for your values?
- Which values cause you anxiety? Why? What does this tell you?

Let's now turn our attention to a practical consideration. Our wants and values are often intertwined in a behavioral lattice which makes it difficult for us to be able to define precisely which of these two is motivating us at any given time. But, is it important to know specifically which of the two it is? And is it possible to even accurately differentiate between them, in the moment? Let's take for example the following 12 dimensions:

Achievement	Belonging	Creativity
Curiosity	Independence	Mastery
Power	Wealth	Prestige
Security	Service	Structure

Examining any of these closely, we can see that they can alternate roles, depending on our circumstances. Take "Achievement": it can be a want, or a value—even a need. In any of these cases, it will propel us to some action and in some cases, to the very same action regardless of how we label it. It can motivate us, for example, to set stretch goals, to value the achievement itself over the monetary compensation for it and to seek others' approval. Take another example: "Belonging." No matter what descriptive tag we add to it, it will motivate some thoughts, emotional states or actions, such as, feeling good in the company of others and wanting to collaborate and cooperate with them. The same can be said of every dimension on this list.

There is clearly no great value added in being adept at ascertaining the exact nature of these motivators. Leaders don't stop in the middle of their day to check-in on the right label for the motivator of the moment. What is important, however, is to be aware of these motivators in action, to be able to recognize when they are in play in our life. In addition to being aware of their manifestation, we need to be able to understand the impact that they have on our thoughts, feelings, behaviors and actions. By recognizing the powerful influence of these motivators, you can use them to your advantage—to fuel you and propel you forward to the achievement of your goals, or to help you to nimbly skirt around them when they turn into disadvantages or obstacles in your course.

Your wants (and needs) and values are the nexus of your leadership persona. Knowing them intimately is like concentrating a light into a coherent beam with laser-like precision and clarity. We find that a path of simplicity emerges out of our personal chaos when we take the time to understand these three powerful motivators. And because you ultimately control all three, you can influence these motivations to your best advantage by being able to make more informed decisions when they each vie for satisfaction and in so doing, clearing up energy and space for you.

The motivation to lead does not come from external sources. It's the by-product of your desire to lead, your passion to accomplish something of value and your intense belief in your ability to realize these accomplishments. It stems from an innate passionate sense of your potential as a leader. Finally, it's about your internal clarity on why you chose to lead. Motivation is an inside job.

LEADERSHIP EXPLORATIONS
A Fire Within: The Power of Motivation

Listed below are ten drivers that influence individuals, in varying degrees, to assume leadership roles. Consider what each of these drivers means for you and the influence it has on your motivation to lead. Rank these drivers in the order of influence on you and your leadership. *(1= the most influence; 10 = the least influence)*

Drivers	Rank Order (1–10)
Financial	
Achievement	
Recognition	
Relationships	
Development	
Security	
Service	
Contribution	
Innovation	
Structure	

What is the most significant opportunity facing you today? How might that opportunity be realized with more effective leadership?

_____

_____

_____
_____
_____
_____
_____
_____
_____
_____

What is the most significant challenge facing you today? How might this challenge be overcome with more effective leadership?

_____
_____
_____
_____
_____
_____
_____

How does your leadership affect ...
• your team?
• your organization?
• your community?
• your family?
• your customers?

Write a paragraph that describes the ways in which your life is better when you choose to lead.

_____
_____
_____

_____

_____

_____

_____

_____

_____

_____

_____

Reflect on your answers to the previous questions and craft a personal credo that answers the question: "Why do you lead?"

My Motivation Credo is ...

_____

_____

_____

_____

_____

_____

_____

_____

_____

_____

_____

_____

_____

_____

_____

_____

_____

_____

_____

_____

_____

_____

INTERVIEW

A Fire Within: The Power of Motivation

Thomas W. Steipp
President & Chief Executive Officer
Symmetricom, Inc.

I am asked sometimes why I choose to be in a leadership role considering the challenge of leading in today's organizations which are complex, diverse, chaotic, and continually changing. This desire to lead goes back to either my genes or my early training. I was exposed to many examples of good leadership in my early formative years. From a relatively early age, we need input from our parents and I received that encouragement. I was also in Eagle Scouts and in the military—both of these organizations place a premium on leadership. Did this help in my motivation to lead or was it more naturally in my genes? I really can't tell you for sure which had the greater influence.

The impetus to lead is something that has to come from within: People have to want the ball and want to take the shot. People who truly want to lead are more comfortable doing that. Others, on the other hand, like to be a part of a team, to be number two and prefer that. For most of my experience, leading up to my current position, I have gravitated to leadership roles. It's been a natural pull for me.

There are leaders who are thrust into leadership positions, who did not seek to lead. If you are an emergent leader who finds himself in this situation and who doesn't want to lead, my advice would be to find your replacement quickly. Sometimes, you may have been the best alternative for a leadership position, but if you don't have the passion, if you are not willing to study, not willing to make mistakes and learn from your mistakes, you will ultimately not succeed as a leader, for the long-term.

There are, of course, many extrinsic reasons such as remuneration, bonuses and other perks that keep people in leadership positions, regardless of whether they want to lead or not. For sure, these are strong motivations that might keep one in a leadership position, but, to put it in biblical terms: "Without vision, the people will perish." This is absolutely the case in leadership. So, if you are in it just for the extrinsic reasons and don't have a vision for your team, for your organization, then you are on a slippery path. Any organization that has no view for something better, for its customers and employees, is a bad place to work.

I enjoy working with teams, I have a burning vision to grow a company and I enjoy being a part of success. Success in business can be defined in many ways—for me, it's Growth and Profit. If you can't have Growth and Profit, the work of a chief executive officer is not much fun. Unless you simply like being in control and at the top. But leadership is not about control. It's about getting people excited about accomplishing objectives that they may have not otherwise attempted.

If your motivation to lead is external, it's not as powerful as an internal motivation. You may succeed because you may have innate skills that will allow you to be successful, but you will not be as successful as you would be if you had an internal motivation to lead. The fuel is internal. The external part is after the fact; it's the reinforcement.

Having said this, there are often difficult moments in everyone's leadership journey and during those challenging times, we need something to strengthen our motivation, to give us that extra push to stay the course. For me, this comes from feedback from employees and from customers ... from the Board. The feedback that gives you that motive to overcome the net obstacles, to overcome those periods of doubt, periods when things do not go well, when you make mistakes ... all these things happen. If you let these things dominate you, then you are not made for leadership unless your motivation is external and it is so strong that you say: I have to keep doing it.

I can think of specific instances when this type of feedback had an impact on me to renew my energy and continue my work as a leader. Such instances involve employees who over the years have sent me letters saying things such as: "Gosh, I really enjoyed it when you were here. I appreciate what you did to help me." It doesn't happen very often—there are two or three times when guys sent letters to me. I have also had fellows sit down and say: "I appreciate what you are doing for the company and how you do it."

Other things that keep me in the game at times of difficulty and challenge are the integrity of the team, for one. Being focused on innovation is another—innovation is better than competition. Customers who trust you are also a key factor for me.

If you have these three aspects—team integrity, innovation, and your customers' trust—they sustain your motivation to lead. If you have breaches in any of these aspects, you find yourself in a rut. You need to ensure that customers trust you so feedback from people in the organization who are close to customers is critical. But you also need to develop a cadre of safe consultants who will give you very direct feedback, which includes the negative aspects. Any leaders who think that they don't do negative stuff, have not looked at themselves in the mirror—really looked in the mirror. You need to foster an environment where people are willing to receive that type of feedback.

Now, there are times when there are breaches of integrity. When this happens, a leader needs to reflect on why it happened. If you get lapses in your team, in your organization, you have to ask yourself: what's causing that? Are you perhaps putting so much pressure on people that it gets them to do wrong things? Are you not spending enough time with them, not paying attention to small details, the little things that let small lapses go unaddressed? Often, they are very little but they pave the way to further breaches.

Leadership, when done right, is a highly rewarding experience despite the hard work and stress associated with the journey. I feel best about myself as a leader when the team works well, when the organization is profitable and growing, when we are doing the right things, as opposed to expedient things. And the "right things" are not always obvious. When the vision and values are clear and the level of consensus is high, when the team is able to prevail against difficult odds, then it is easy to feel good as a leader. If, on the other hand, I am doing all the right things, but the company is not growing and is not profitable, then I can't feel good as a leader, or, even if the company is growing and is profitable, but the teams are fighting and there are no clear values and vision, then it would be difficult for me to feel good as a leader. The Board and investors would be happy, but even if the Board and investors are happy, I would not feel good if the other components are not in place.

Given that a leader's job has inherent stress associated with it, you need to develop strategies to counter that, to renew yourself. For me, what counteracts the stress is a focus on integrity and making sure that customers trust you. I strongly believe that innovation has to be a part of the equation, of the cycle of renewal—always. It's pretty easy to fall into a rut, otherwise. A friend of mine used to say that a rut is nothing more than a coffin with the ends kicked out. Innovation is everybody's objective—but how do you do it? How do you find ways to stay fresh? One way is to read great books, spend time with great people, and dream great dreams.

People sometimes ask me what books I would recommend for leadership. Well, there are so many good ones that it would be like voting in a beauty contest. Some that I found particularly useful myself are the trilogy of Jim Collins' books: Good to Great, Built to Last *and* Beyond Entrepreneurship.

Jack Welch's book Winning *is also a good one. The key is to figure out what kind of a leader you want to be and then figure out what books will be useful. Read a lot. In some books, you might find nothing that is particularly useful to you, in other books you will find yourself highlighting a lot of passages.*

Leadership fascinates me—not just how to lead, but what's beyond it. Assuming that it's not in your genes, what can you do to be a great leader? What are different things you can do to get better at it? If you are a modest talent, you will be effective at it if you read great books and associate with great people. Don't do an inventory to discover your innate talents. Instead, put your face to the mirror and do a brutal assessment and say, "This is who I am and this is what I have to do to get better." So it starts from the core of who you are.

It's like teaching—the best teachers adapt their style to different students. You must have a core that doesn't change but also have an internal clutch that does change depending on people or circumstances in your environment.

CHAPTER TWO

Perception, Faith, and Self-Limitation

The Power of Your Beliefs

"Man is what he believes."

ANTON CHEKHOV

"Belief," said Samuel Butler, "like any other moving body, follows the path of least resistance." Our system of beliefs functions like an invisible compass that guides us through well-worn pathways and shortcuts, to immediate reactions, decisions, thoughts, actions and emotions. Like an old trusted friend, these beliefs produce in us feelings of ease and security. They make our lives manageable. Interpreting the world around us in light of what we already know is much more expedient than having to constantly ponder the meaning of incoming data and events. Our belief system is really a big part of who we are and how we approach leadership. How clear are your beliefs? How do they influence your interactions with others? Do you have any beliefs that need to be tested? Are there ways in which your belief system can add power to your personal leadership?

Leaders can effectively explore their beliefs by examining their personal schemas, also known as cognitive maps. These are those deeply entrenched beliefs, or set of precepts, that we have about the world around us. For example, if we see a car approaching us on the road and the driver is flashing the high beams, we automatically interpret this as a warning that there is a speed trap ahead. This is a schema that we have constructed from past experience or from what others have told us. So, schemas are often used mental processes that we have developed over many years to interpret our experiences and the actions of others. Scholars at Yale University compare these habitual patterns of thinking, feeling, and acting to a "well-maintained, multi-lane, high-speed, super-highway—fast, convenient, and readily accessed—moving us rapidly, automatically ... a super-highway of interconnected thoughts, feelings, and behaviors." They reflect not only our beliefs about the world around us but also our self-schemas, the beliefs we have about ourselves which define who we are.

For example, some of us may believe that we are very likeable while others among us may believe that we are not so likeable. Some of us may believe that our success as leaders is due to our hard work while others may believe that it is due to nothing more than good luck. Schemas can be positive or negative. They can be an accurate or inaccurate reflection of reality. One thing is certain—these mental frameworks are so central to our identity that we usually resist changing them and they may significantly limit our possibilities as a leader. Schemas are frequently referred to as life traps—they shape our life's viewpoints and experiences. Anton Chekhov said it best: "Man is what he believes."

So what are the implications of your personal schema system in terms of your leadership power? Let's explore this question as it applies to a most important area of leadership—your view of yourself. When new information does not fit an existing schema, we simply discount it or it quickly leaves our memory. Our schemas can therefore easily block our motivation to learn something new about ourselves. This can lessen the opportunities for us to sharpen our focus on how we really are when we function at our best. Beliefs can close our minds. Moreover, schemas affect what we recall and we can therefore shortchange ourselves from attending to useful information about ourselves. Schemas also place labels on all that is important to us; faulty schemas can result in inaccurate labels. Worn-out schemas that belonged to our past life also can cause rigidity and a lack of flexibility to incorporate new information that can help us evolve to be at our leading edge. We become stuck and our self-schemas become self-perpetuating and self-sustaining. Finally, self-schemas act as powerful filters, affecting where we focus our attention.

Indeed, self-schemas have a very profound influence on how we view ourselves. They either propel us forward or hold us back, depending on the nature of the schemas. Here are some examples:

- If we think we are courageous, we are more likely to take risks.
- If we think we are good presenters, we are more likely to seek opportunities to speak in public.
- If we think we're "not good with people," we are more likely to limit the number of personal interactions with others.
- If we believe that one has to do something right the first time, we may not try innovative solutions.
- If we believe that we have the power to solve our own problems, we become more self-reliant and less outwardly dependant.

Once we start to become aware of our self-schemas, we are better able to create boundaries between our various self-images. So, an unfavorable image in one aspect of ourselves would not spread beyond its boundary to taint other areas of our sense of self-worth.

Another important component of self-schemas consists of the mental images we have of our own histories. These can be a source of power and pride for us—a sense of our values and accomplishments. There is much leadership strength to be gained in constructing and maintaining a large library of such positive self-images. The other side of the coin is that these images, if negative, can become anchors that limit our actions if we don't face them and relegate them to just what they are: our past selves, not who we are today. Our historic schemas can greatly impact our present leadership actions. This can have a significant influence on what we believe we are capable of doing. A leader's schemas need to be examined and ruthlessly confronted. Perhaps this is one interpretation we could attribute to Socrates' famous words: "The unexamined life is not worth living." This is a key point. It is through engaging in inquiry and rejecting blind acceptance of past schemas about who we are, that we become the leader we do not yet believe we can be.

We also need to ask ourselves if there are areas where we are "aschematic," i.e., where we do not have a schema for a particular dimension. It can be a source of great inspiration to know that there is a part of us that is untouched by anything we have ever done before. We can approach this area as a *tabula rasa,* without limitations, without boundaries, a beautiful clean slate waiting to be written on— something akin to the philosopher John Locke's concept of the young mind not yet affected by experience. Are there such dimensions in your life, in your career as a leader? In which unexplored territories can you venture to spread your leadership wings?

What are your habitual self-schemas? What impact do they have on your behavior? In other words, to borrow again the metaphor from Yale University: If your schemas are a super highway, where are they taking you? Are they transporting you automatically, mindlessly, through each day? Are they preventing you from fully expressing and pursuing your highest ideals?

Do your self-schemas match how you want to present yourself to the communities in which you lead? If not, how do they differ from the way you see yourself?

Are there any self-schemas which are consistently manifested in all your roles? Or are there any that show up only in certain contexts? What insights does this give you?

Are there any schemas that belong to a past self? Are they positive or negative? If they are negative, can you dispute them? Can you act as your own defense lawyer? How can you clear the slate of these power robbers?

What schemas have crystallized into habits that don't serve you well? What schemas have been particularly beneficial to you in your relationship with others? How can you leverage these positive schemas more often?

In the process of answering these questions, of creating an inventory of your schemas and analyzing their worth to you, you become more conscious of them. They act like a pop-up dialog box, reminding you when you are about to take an action. You become more mindful and you are then in a position to select your behavior or feeling about a particular situation. You're no longer acting from impulse. Understanding our schemas and controlling them frees us from their bond and gives us clarity to see fresh choices. It's a very rewarding journey.

LEADERSHIP EXPLORATIONS

Perception, Faith, and Self-Limitation: The Power of Your Beliefs

Complete the following statements thoroughly and honestly. Please leave a, b, and c blank at this time.

Leaders develop best when _____.

a. _____

b. _____

c. _____

The most important leadership competency is _____.

Organizations can be best described as _____
_____.

a. _____

b. _____

c. _____

I am at my best as a leader when _____
_____.

a. _____

b. _____

c. _____

Organizational culture can be most effectively changed by _____
_____.

a. _____

b. _____

c. _____

The most important personal traits of a leader are _____
_____.

a. _____

b. _____

c. _____

My weakest aspects as a leader include _____
_____.
a. _____
b. _____
c. _____

To change a team, leaders must focus on_____
_____.
a. _____
b. _____
c. _____

Poor performers are usually_____
_____.
a. _____
b. _____
c. _____

My future as a leader will include _____
_____.
a. _____
b. _____
c. _____

Now review what you wrote and consider your personal beliefs associated with these statements and answer the following questions for each:

a. In what ways might this belief serve or add to your leadership effectiveness?

b. In what ways might this belief limit your leadership effectiveness?

c. What is a completely different perspective?

CHAPTER THREE

I Am *Really* OK
The Power of Self-Acceptance

*"Our deepest fear is not that we are inadequate.
Our deepest fear is that we are powerful beyond measure.
It is our light that most frightens us. We ask ourselves,
'Who am I to be brilliant, gorgeous, talented and
fabulous?' Actually, who are you not to be?"*

MARIANNE WILLIAMSON

Artists will often make numerous rough sketches of their final composition before putting brush to canvas. When we look at these sketches, we know they are simply preludes to the final masterpiece. We don't judge the sketch negatively because it is incomplete. We know that it is a work in progress. The same applies to us, as leaders. No one assumes the mantle of leadership fully equipped for this demanding role. Even the greatest leaders are a painting in progress. At its most basic level, self-acceptance means understanding this fundamental point about leadership and about being human. We are all continuously evolving and changing, and coming to grips with this fact is a source of great strength. A lack of self-acceptance as leaders has a detrimental effect on our level of energy, on our approach to performance and achievement and, ultimately, on the enjoyment of the journey. Leaders gain great power when they accept their imperfections as inescapable and as opportunities for personal development, as opposed to permanent deficits.

A lack of self-acceptance can be a troublesome obstacle for all of us, but it is often pervasive for newly-minted leaders faced with the daunting task of establishing their own leadership brand. What causes us to reject ourselves? Sometimes, it is simply a new challenge for which we feel unprepared. On a deeper level, this lack of self-acceptance has emotional roots that began long before we embarked on our leadership mission—roots grounded in childhood experiences of not always being accepted as who we were by parents, caregivers, or teachers. Lack of self-acceptance is something that starts in childhood and we learn to internalize it over a lifetime. As leaders, it is particularly important that we unlearn any lack of self-acceptance that we may have internalized.

As odd as this seems, we gain leadership power when we acknowledge the negative aspects of ourselves and become comfortable with these demons. This helps us gain clarity on how we may be blinded by situations and how we may be magnifying negatives. This realization, frees us of these emotional hooks. Try this: List every possible item about yourself that you don't like. Then ask yourself: "So what?" This is a moment in your stage of evolution, a phase in your painting in progress. It's a painting undergoing normal stages of creation until it is completed. Instead of seeing yourself as an imperfect painting, we encourage you to see yourself as a magnificent work of art awaiting the finishing touches.

It is important to note that we are not advocating blind self-acceptance. Instead, we are encouraging self-determination. Be deliberate about who you want to be. Be purposeful about the look of your finished leadership portrait. Eleanor Roosevelt said: "I think that somehow, we learn who we really are, and then live with that decision." One of the hallmarks of great leaders is that they decide who they will be as a leader. They do not leave this important task in the care of their own inner critics. They know that a lack of strengths in one area does not override strengths in another area. They don't dwell on their limitations. They accept that one day they may function well in one dimension, and that on another day, they may not function as well in the very same dimension. They recognize their limitations but they do not let them tarnish their self-image. Self-acceptance is very closely tied to self-image. No matter what events conspire to derail their plans, no matter what personal weakness may result in a less than perfect execution, great leaders don't let this erode their self-image. They maintain their strength and belief in themselves through hope, positivism and optimism. Leaders are in fact merchants of hope, and they inspire themselves and others with a positive outlook. They are mindful not to view themselves in a negative manner and thereby diminish their leadership power. They meet their demons, embracing them head on.

Powerful leaders are also comfortable with the notion that risk accompanies potential failure. When they make a mistake or fail, they don't think badly of themselves. They don't accept themselves *despite* their weaknesses–they accept themselves–period. They know that they are not their behavior, that they are more than the sum total of their traits and actions–good or bad–and that it is impossible, therefore, to rate themselves accurately. As Albert Ellis said: "Our essence is determined by millions of acts, deeds, and traits during our lifetime. It is, therefore, impossible to base our self-acceptance on a notion that we can accurately sum up who we are."

These great leaders, however, focus on one thing: operating from the standpoint of their giftedness–a powerful platform, indeed. These people are not manipulated externally but always operate from an internal locus of control, approving of themselves. They don't wait for the trumpet call from outside. They pursue accomplishments not to prove their worth to others, but for the joy of achieving something of significance. So their self-acceptance is not tied to what others think of them. They are therefore freed of much of the tyranny of the other and can focus on what they want to accomplish without the weight and pressure of others' validation. Self-acceptance then leads to independence and independence is a major contributor to leadership power.

A strong sense of self-acceptance also aids in establishing a leader's authenticity with others in the organization. It means not having to work on hiding or compensating for parts of ourselves so that we are always behaving in grace and harmony with the essence of who we are. We show up as genuine, comfortable in our skin. If you want to be a powerful force in any circumstance, then there is no better way than being yourself, making the most of your best. Creativity also flourishes when we accept ourselves as we attain greater peace of mind and release blocked energies to focus on possibilities instead of being drained by self-rejection. Self-acceptance is also a powerful source of strength as it gives us the confidence to stand up for our values and principles and defend them even when confronted by strong opposition. It also gives us the power to acknowledge when we are wrong.

A salient characteristic of self-accepting people is that they tend to live in the moment. They are not immobilized by the mistakes or faults of the past, and they don't let these temporary setbacks color the potentialities of the future. They are free to be fully in the present, to enjoy the powerful state of control and mindfulness which makes them more effective as leaders.

Finally, self-acceptance is about not being afraid of your greatness. It's about using all of your talents and gifts to the maximum, without reticence or apology, and embracing your full life as a leader. True greatness "lets itself be touched and handled, it loses nothing by being seen at close quarters."[2] Our lives are shaped by our minds; we become what we think. What is the image you hold of yourself? What kind of leader do you believe yourself to be? Are you aware of the recurring self-perceptions that you have created? Do these support a positive, strong image of you as a capable and potent leader? What steps can you take immediately to deliberately determine who you want to be? What aspects of that portrait need to be added, completed, refined, or repainted? Is there anything that you need to airbrush? Self-acceptance is a gift we give to ourselves. It's the gift of self-trust. We encourage you to make self-trust a life-long habit. Self-acceptance promotes expansiveness, not contraction. Imagine a self-determined "you"—one that comes from a position of abundance and possibilities. Imagine the vast door that would open up in your world, a powerful new level of being—not measuring yourself up against anyone else but yourself—the self that you decide to be, competing only with your personal best. We become very attractive when we embark on this journey of self-acceptance and self-determination, when we choose to operate from our self-selected characteristics, as the basis for a remarkable personality.

LEADERSHIP EXPLORATIONS

I Am *Really* OK: The Power of Self-Acceptance

What do you admire most about others? Consider the positive traits and characteristics of the following people:

	Positive Traits & Characteristics of This Person
Martin Luther King	
Mahatma Gandhi	
Mother Teresa	
Jack Welch	
Bill Gates	
Steve Jobs	
Your Mother	
Your Father	
An Effective Teacher	
A Great Coach	
A Respected Manager	
A Close Friend	
A Trusted Politician	

Consider all the ways you are like each of these individuals:

	Ways I Am Like This Person
Martin Luther King	
Mahatma Gandhi	
Mother Teresa	
Jack Welch	
Bill Gates	
Steve Jobs	
Your Mother	
Your Father	
An Effective Teacher	
A Great Coach	
A Respected Manager	
A Close Friend	
A Trusted Politician	

My Leadership Résumé

Using the previous exercise as your inspiration, create an advertisement (words, images, models, etc.) that describes you, at your best, as a leader.

_____

_____

_____

_____

_____

_____

_____

_____

_____

_____

_____

_____

_____

_____

_____

_____

_____

_____

_____

_____

_____

_____

_____

_____

_____

_____

_____

_____

_____

INTERVIEW

I Am *Really* OK: The Power of Self-Acceptance

Brian Traquair
President
SunGard, Capital Markets and Investment Banking

What I have observed in leadership and management is that people who understand themselves and accept who they are—the good and the bad—are more honest with their staff, more relaxed, and not as appearance-driven. By virtue of that acceptance, they have better relationships—they are not victims of ego trips or other ways of proving that they are tall, smart, or handsome. When you choose between looking good and making others look good, it's a mistake. One of the lines I use is: "Seldom to blame, but always responsible." It's my way of saying that we have to take responsibility no matter what and stand up for the team.

The mistakes I have made are typically those times I tried to show people how smart I am—when I didn't know where we needed to go but I didn't engage with others, didn't state that fact, and did not ask for help. Self-acceptance is about liking who you are and coming to terms with who you are becoming. People who have a lot to prove to others make ineffective, often difficult managers—and they do not inspire others to follow.

I am accepted in my workplace for who I am. People who work with me know that I do my best work and that I don't pretend. Beyond the business world, I am loved and accepted at home, and I am lucky to be part of a great neighborhood and church community. This acceptance and belonging is the foundation for everything else I am able to do.

When I am in situations where I am not known or accepted, I start with education—people fear what they don't understand. I have hundreds of people in my business, who have never met me—so I have conversations. I had three such conversations just today with people in Europe whom I do not know. I tell people about myself and ask them about themselves. I tell them what I think of a situation, and they tell me what they think. But if you just do this to get people on your side, it won't work. If you are honest, people notice it and appreciate it. It leads to trust. If you genuinely say: "I didn't know a few weeks ago that I would have this promotion," people are stunned. When something happens, people often say: "It doesn't surprise me." Well, things regularly surprise me and I am generally closer to the news and our future plans. They must be clairvoyants. As a leader, when you let on that you are surprised, or overjoyed, you let others see more of the person behind the title. It's about authenticity. I don't know how to lead people without authenticity. And authenticity comes from self-acceptance. In contrast, managers who are unhappy with who they are or who don't accept themselves, are often unable to build the trust needed to lead.

So, when do I disappoint myself? When I don't have the courage to do what I need to do. For example, when someone I am working with tells me that an individual is creating problems. I should deal with it directly. I fail when I do not meet with them personally and say: "I understand there is a problem." If I procrastinate or hide behind my intermediate manager, knowing full well that I should be dealing with it myself, then I disappoint myself. The same is true of confrontations and seemingly impossible problems—I am disappointed with myself when I do not have the energy and courage to engage.

Another time when I disappoint myself is when vanity gets in the way. We all carry around us a sense of ego and self worth—to get us through the typically long days as leaders. But if you draw some attention to your success, more than is warranted, you take away from your team. There are those who give credit to others publicly—but if you listen to private conversation, the "I" comes up in their description of accomplishments. The words we say in private are really a reflection of what's going on in our brain; they are what we are thinking. If you really want to know how you are perceived as a leader, you should listen in to the supper conversations of your team members with their partners. In 30 seconds you will know everything you needed, good and bad—how much credit you give and take is guaranteed to be part of that conversation.

If I were to say when it is that I am particularly proud of myself, it would be when I hire or promote the right person when it is not obvious that he or she is the right choice—when I see something in someone that makes me believe, and I take the chance to move that individual out of relative obscurity into a higher profile project or role. For example, it might be someone from customer service who has the right attitude, who can inspire others, who is articulate - giving them the opportunity to play on a bigger stage as a manager or leader. Some become more than I dreamed possible.

In choosing people, we leave a legacy. In choosing people, we articulate our beliefs and from that, people infer what is important to us. Failure is when we promote our favorite people or the most popular ones and lose the respect of our teams. Failure is when we don't let go of the people in the wrong position because we don't have firsthand evidence of reasons. We need to be conscious that, as leaders, we are often the last ones to know and yet the first ones to be judged. We must rely on choosing the right people and not the favorites, relying on your managers, your contacts, objective measurements, and two-way communication and reviews.

Self-acceptance is a journey. There is value in experience and wisdom. If we look at people in their 20s and 30s, they often do not know who they are or who they want to become, so they are not as effective as someone who has journeyed farther, accepted himself or herself, and knows that one person can't be all things to all people.

Self-acceptance is also tied to balance. Balance for me, is based on four pillars—family, work, community, and church. My goal is to be engaged in all of these areas in a balanced way. It is the hardest thing I do (and I am not alone). I believe that I become a better leader because I participate in outside work. I have the opportunity to learn about myself in a different setting and with different types of people. Individuals who only focus on work get only one view through the lens of life—it is much more effective and rewarding to see the world in many different perspectives. I learn more about myself when I engage with people and organizations outside of work—that's where I get more truth because people at work are naturally more guarded. To be a better leader, you need to hear the truth about yourself.

CHAPTER FOUR

An Angel and a Madman

The Power of Your Personality

"I hold a beast, an angel, and a madman in me, and my enquiry is as to their working, and my problem is their subjugation and victory, downthrow and upheaval, and my effort is their self-expression."

DYLAN THOMAS

While your approach to leadership is greatly influenced by deeply held beliefs, values, and aspirations, those you lead experience you primarily through your personality. Think of your personality as a colorful amalgam of all of those traits and characteristics, both good and bad, that others see. These factors play a large role in shaping your interpersonal behavior, in setting your personal priorities and influencing how you organize your life. The manifestation of your personality will also have a significant effect on your personal leadership brand throughout your career. Gaining a deep understanding of one's personality is one of the most important facets of self-awareness and is well worth the extensive exploration. Leaders who are armed with this profound self-knowledge are able to readily capitalize on their natural strengths while lessening the potential negative impact in areas of vulnerability.

39

Personality traits are generally assumed to be stable over time, that is, they persist throughout our life and constitute our true nature. While this is likely true, an overly narrow interpretation may lead to the risky assumption that the fundamental aspects of our personalities are immutable and unchangeable and that our patterns of behavior are carved in stone. Maybe even more importantly, this assumption may prevent us from looking beyond our easily recognized attributes, beyond those well-practiced behaviors that are so natural to us, to see the less expressed traits, those hidden and perhaps undiscovered dimensions of ourselves. This is an area that holds rich development opportunities for the leader.

As you examine your leadership palette, you are encouraged to take a wide-angle view of all of your possible personality traits. This needs to be very intentional. Many of us structure our everyday, non-work lives so that we rarely encounter the circumstances that will elicit the less visible and more neglected parts of our personalities. We lean toward the comfort of our well-known selves. On the other hand, the intensity and unpredictability of organization life provides the leader limitless opportunities for self-discovery. How frequently and thoroughly do you study yourself? Do you make note of how you respond to conflict or how you make decisions? Consider how some of your traits may be situational. Are they conspicuously absent in other situations? In what situations do you feel particularly potent, decisive and fully engaged? When do you feel weak and powerless? How can you use these insights to increase your effectiveness as a leader?

We cannot view personality in black and white terms—it is much more accurately depicted as a spectrum of colors with varying hues and tints. An oversimplification of personality theory may lead us to think of our traits in bipolar terms, that is, we are assumed to have one trait or its opposite. For example, we might see ourselves as exclusively extraverted or introverted. The reality is, however, that personality traits occur along a continuum. Knowledge of where we naturally reside on that continuum and what causes us to slide from one end to the other is the key to the leader's self-awareness and self-management.

Are all personality traits equal? Researchers believe that our behavior is largely influenced by cardinal traits.[3] A cardinal trait is the most important component of your personality, that which dominates your personality in all contexts and across time. It is so dominant that there are few actions you undertake that would not be traced to its influence, whether directly or indirectly. Do you have a cardinal trait, one that dominates all of your interpersonal interactions? Does it narrow or expand your repertoire of leadership behaviors? Do you control it or does it control you?

Not all of our personality traits are positive and there may be parts of us that are in direct opposition of each other. We can be both slothful and energetic, stubborn and yielding, sensitive and tough minded, all in one. We need to embrace this duality as part of our mosaic—all the small pieces of color that are a composite of our personality. The darker traits are an integral part of who we are, and in many cases, help us and others to appreciate our positive parts—just as we know darkness from knowing light, joy from knowing grief, and harmony from knowing dissonance. Approaching our leadership self-portrait with a view to eliminating or suppressing parts of ourselves that we may feel don't fit our current roles would be akin to a film editor cutting out any scene containing strife or pain from a movie. When we do this, we dilute our authentic self and we lose our personal power.

There is also an inner and outer dimension to personality. The innermost part of us is the person we believe we truly are and encompasses all of the traits and characteristics we believe we possess. The outer part, on the other hand, is how our personality translates into patterns of behaviors that are seen and judged by others—in short, our reputations. The gap between these two dimensions is perhaps one of the most fertile areas for self-discovery and growth.

In the past century, several theories of personality have been developed, each with their own taxonomy of traits and characteristics. These theories and associated taxonomies can serve leaders as valuable starting points as they seek to learn more about their distinctive personality palettes. Following is a synopsis of four, widely-accepted personality models that are particularly useful for leadership development: the *Big Five Model,* the *FIRO-B® Model,* the *16 Personality Factors Model,* and the *Myers-Briggs Personality Inventory™ Model.*

PERSONALITY MODELS

The Big Five Model

This five-factor model, also referred to by the acronym OCEAN, comprises five bi-polar personality dimensions of Extraversion, Neuroticism, Openness to Experience, Agreeableness, and Conscientiousness. These five dimensions are considered by many psychologists to be the most complete description of personality.

Extraversion	Neuroticism	Openness to Experience	Agreeableness	Conscientiousness
Warmth	Anxiety	Fantasy	Trust	Competence
Gregariousness	Angry hostility	Aesthetics	Straightforwardness	Order
Assertiveness	Depression	Feelings	Altruism	Dutifulness
Activity	Self-consciousness	Actions	Compliance	Achievement striving
Excitement-seeking	Impulsiveness	Ideas	Modesty	Self-discipline
Positive emotions	Vulnerability	Values	Tendermindedness	Deliberation

Chart Source: *The Big Five Trait Categories* (Costa & McRae, 1994). Cited by William Todd Schultz in *Handbook of Psychobiography*. USA: Oxford University Press, 2005). All rights reserved.

Being aware of which personality dimensions drive you is a powerful tool to help you discover how you show up in leadership situations. Perhaps more importantly, it would help you to decide which leadership situations would prove stressful so that you can make contingency behavioral plans that would allow you to always be in your power.

The FIRO-B® (Fundamental Interpersonal Relations Orientation–Behavior) Model

William C. Shutz created the FIRO-B® instrument which measures three fundamental dimensions of interpersonal relations: Inclusion (Recognition, Belonging and Participation), Control (Influence, Leading and Responsibility) and Affection (Closeness, Warmth and Sensitivity), on two dimensions of behavior: Expressed and Wanted. The Expressed behavior refers to the extent to which we initiate actions while the Wanted behavior refers to the extent to which we prefer to be the recipients of actions.

This instrument reveals how we behave toward others and our expectations of others in terms of their behavior toward us. It helps us understand the impact that our personal needs have on any actions we undertake.

Inclusion	Control	Affection
Expressed How much effort you make to include others in your activities. How much effort you put in trying to belong, to join social groups, and to be with others as much as possible.	*Expressed* Your need to exert control and influence over things. Your enjoyment of organizing things and directing others.	*Expressed* The extent to which you are comfortable expressing personal feelings and trying to be supportive of others.
Wanted How much you want other people to include you in their activities and to invite you to belong. Your level of enjoyment when others notice you.	*Wanted* The extent to which you feel comfortable working in well-defined situations. The extent to which you try to get clear expectations and instructions.	*Wanted* Your need for others to act warmly toward you. The extent to which you enjoy it when people share their feelings with you and when they encourage your efforts.

Chart Source: *FIRO-B® Interpretative Report for Organizations.* CPP Inc. All rights reserved.

The 16 Personality Factors (PF)

The 16PF assesses personality against 16 primary personality factors. The 16 traits are on a continuum; we all have some degree of every trait. The assessment determines where on the continuum we fall.

Descriptors of Low Range	Primary Factor	Descriptors of High Range
Impersonal, distant, cool, reserved, detached, formal, aloof	Warmth	Warm, outgoing, attentive to others, kindly, easy going, participating, likes people
Concrete thinking, lower general mental capacity, less intelligent, unable to handle abstract problems	Reasoning	Abstract-thinking, more intelligent, bright, higher general mental capacity, fast learner
Reactive emotionally, changeable, affected by feelings, emotionally less stable, easily upset	Emotional Stability	Emotionally stable, adaptive, mature, faces reality calmly
Deferential, cooperative, avoids conflict, submissive, humble, obedient, easily led, docile, accommodating	Dominance	Dominant, forceful, assertive, aggressive, competitive, stubborn, bossy
Serious, restrained, prudent, taciturn, introspective, silent	Liveliness	Lively, animated, spontaneous, enthusiastic, happy-go-lucky, cheerful, expressive, impulsive (Surgency)

Descriptors of Low Range	Primary Factor	Descriptors of High Range
Expedient, nonconforming, disregards rules, self indulgent	Rule-Consciousness	Rule-conscious, dutiful, conscientious, conforming, moralistic, staid, rule-bound
Shy, threat-sensitive, timid, hesitant, intimidated	Social Boldness	Socially bold, venturesome, thick-skinned, uninhibited
Utilitarian, objective, unsentimental, tough-minded, self-reliant, no-nonsense, rough	Sensitivity	Sensitive, aesthetic, sentimental, tender-minded, intuitive, refined
Trusting, unsuspecting, accepting, unconditional, easy	Vigilance	Vigilant, suspicious, skeptical, distrustful, oppositional
Forthright, genuine, artless, open, guileless, naive, unpretentious, involved	Privateness	Private, discreet, non-disclosing, shrewd, polished, worldly, astute, diplomatic
Grounded, practical, prosaic, solution-oriented, steady, conventional	Abstractedness	Abstract, imaginative, absent-minded, impractical, absorbed in ideas
Self-assured, unworried, complacent, secure, free of guilt, confident, self-satisfied	Apprehension	Apprehensive, self-doubting, worried, guilt prone, insecure, worrying, self-blaming

Descriptors of Low Range	Primary Factor	Descriptors of High Range
Traditional, attached to familiar, conservative, respecting traditional ideas	Openness to Change	Open to change, experimental, liberal, analytical, critical, free-thinking, flexibility
Group-oriented, affiliative, a joiner and follower, dependent (group adherence)	Self-Reliance	Self-reliant, solitary, resourceful, individualistic, self-sufficient (Self-Sufficiency)
Tolerated disorder, unexacting, flexible, undisciplined, lax, self-conflict, impulsive, careless of social rules, uncontrolled	Perfectionism	Perfectionist, organized, compulsive, self-disciplined, socially precise, exacting will power, control, self-sentimental
Relaxed, placid, tranquil, torpid, patient, composed, low drive	Tension	Tense, high-energy, impatient, driven, frustrated, overwrought, time driven

Chart Source: *16 PF–Fifth Edition: Technical Manual.* (Conn,, & Rieke, Eds. 1994). Champaign, IL: Institute for Personality and Ability Testing Inc. All rights reserved.

The Myers-Briggs Personality Inventory™ Model

The Myers-Briggs Personality Inventory™ (MBTI) identifies our natural inclinations for certain ways of thinking and behaving, known as preferences. There are four preferences which result in 16 personality types. The four preferences are: where we prefer to direct our energy (extraversion vs. introversion); how we prefer to process information (sensing vs. intuition); how we prefer to make decisions (thinking vs. feeling) and how we prefer to organize our life (judging vs. perceiving).

Extraversion		Introversion	Sensing		Intuition
Initiating	vs.	Receiving	Concrete	vs.	Abstract
Expressive	vs.	Contained	Realistic	vs.	Imaginative
Gregarious	vs.	Intimate	Practical	vs.	Inferential
Participative	vs.	Reflective	Experiential	vs.	Theoretical
Enthusiastic	vs.	Quiet	Traditional	vs.	Original
Thinking		**Feeling**	**Judging**		**Perceiving**
Logical	vs.	Empathetic	Systematic	vs.	Casual
Reasonable	vs.	Compassionate	Planful	vs.	Open-ended
Questioning	vs.	Accommodating	Early Starting	vs.	Pressure-prompted
Critical	vs.	Accepting	Scheduled	vs.	Spontaneous
Tough	vs.	Tender	Methodical	vs.	Emergent

Chart Source: *MBTI™ Step II: Interpretative Report*, CPP Inc. All rights reserved.

Any of the preceding personality instruments are helpful in deepening your knowledge of your personality. Your personality traits are the under painting—that initial layer. Just like the monochrome under painting of a masterful portrait establishes its basic composition before the final color coats and glazes are applied, so your personality is the foundation that drives your personal beliefs, expectations, desires, values and behaviors. This is a powerful dimension for the personal self—the impression we make on others—and nowhere more important than for your leadership persona. As Peter F. Drucker puts it: "Leadership is … the building of a personality beyond its normal limitations."

LEADERSHIP EXPLORATIONS

An Angel and a Madman: The Power of Your Personality

Select 15 words from the following list that best describe your personality and approach to life:

Abstract	Expressive	Personal
Accurate	Flexible	Planned
Action-oriented	Gregarious	Practical
Adaptable	Helpful	Process-oriented
Analytical	Imaginative	Purposeful
Casual	Impersonal	Quiet
Compassionate	Initiator	Realistic
Competitive	Intellectual	Receptive
Confirming	Introspective	Reserved
Contained	Intuitive	Scheduled
Cooperative	Joyful	Sensitive
Creative	Logical	Serious
Critical	Methodical	Skeptical
Decisive	Modest	Spontaneous
Detailed	Objective	Systematic
Disciplined	Observant	Tactful
Easygoing	Open-ended	Theoretical
Emotional	Optimistic	Thoughtful
Empathetic	Organized	Traditional
Energetic	Original	Understanding
Enthusiastic	Passionate	Vocal

Chart Source: Bluepoint Leadership Development, Inc. All rights reserved.

Incorporate the words you selected into ten statements that describe the leadership opportunities inherent in each. Start each sentence with "As a leader, I can use my ..." You may use more than one of the above words in the sentence.

For example:

- *As a leader, I can use my competitive nature and my intuition to create winning strategic plans.*
- *As a leader, I can use my reserved personality, easy-going nature and helpful orientation to build a highly service-oriented, collegial team.*
- *As a leader, I can use my expressive skills and passion to inspire my team.*
- As a leader, I can use my _____

  _____

- As a leader, I can use my _____

  _____

- As a leader, I can use my _____

  _____

- As a leader, I can use my _____

  _____

- As a leader, I can use my _____

  _____

- As a leader, I can use my _____

  _____

- As a leader, I can use my _____

  _____

- As a leader, I can use my _____

  _____

- As a leader, I can use my _____

  _____

- As a leader, I can use my _____

  _____

PART TWO

Your Palette

CHAPTER FIVE

A Gifted Leader

The Power of Valuing Your Strengths

"Nobody ever commented, for example, that the great violinist Jascha Heifetz probably couldn't play the trumpet very well."

PETER F. DRUCKER

Leadership is a challenging path that requires the power that comes from being firmly grounded in your strengths. One of the most frequent causes of leadership failure is not the lack of ability, but rather the leader's preoccupation with his or her weaknesses. Like the rest of us, you have flaws and shortcomings. Leadership is a long and arduous journey and your imperfections will always haunt you to some degree. Maybe you are somewhat unfocused, nervous in large groups, unmotivated in some situations, lacking organization or poor at responding to conflict. As a leader you need to be aware of, and manage, your weaker qualities. However, these need not derail or control you. You seize your power as a leader by focusing primarily on your many natural strengths and talents.

When we focus on our weaknesses, we naturally channel our thoughts toward the possibility of loss and failure and, in so doing, we move from power to powerlessness. We create cracks in our leadership foundation, and slowly, but surely, diminish our faith in our ability to succeed. Paul J. Meyer said: "Enter every activity without giving mental recognition to the possibility of defeat." When we focus on our strengths, we are directing all of our leadership energy toward winning.

The emphasis on weaknesses is a part of our psychological heritage which focuses on curing the ill while ignoring the strengths, finding the deficits, and fixing them. Martin E. Seligman, a psychology pioneer, has been a strong voice advocating that psychology shift its focus from dysfunction to super functioning, and look at the strengths that propel people from normal functioning to outstanding performance.

Most companies under the old-style management practice deficit-thinking which is heavily oriented toward the critical and focusing on discovering what's wrong with people in order to fix them. Thinking back on the traditional performance review system, how many of us had to dig deep to find some areas for improvement to impart to the hapless souls sitting across from us? How many of us, instead, entered this dreaded annual inquisition with a mission to find what propels people to super performance? And do people ever go through a major transformation as a result of the carefully worded feedback on their weak areas? Rarely.

David Cooperrider, the architect of *Appreciative Inquiry,* and Marcus Buckingham, author of *Now, Discover Your Strengths,* have done much to alter the landscape of management by advocating that, contrary to conventional wisdom, great performance comes from appreciating your strengths and not from focusing on your weaknesses. While this is, without a doubt, a positive revolution, we suggest that it does, however, force us to place ourselves on a continuum, reducing us to a linearly ordered set of skills or talents. For example, we are encouraged to see ourselves as either: impulsive or predictable, suspicious or trusting, bold or cautious, altruistic or selfish, candid or reticent, capricious or persistent. But following this polarized thinking does not mirror the human condition which does not place us in pairs of discrete states. We could be all of these dimensions, not either/or. These could all be aspects of ourselves that manifest themselves under different circumstances.

There is a multiplicity of rich threads woven into the complex fabric of our humanity. This is the brilliant tapestry at our core that defines our ethos, our essence. It is an amalgam of our experiences, characteristics, talents, strengths and weaknesses, and a myriad of other aspects. When we are able to bring this entire tapestry to our work, we access our full reservoir of leadership power. When we are shackled by the labels and definitions of what we are good at and what we are not, we discount this powerful amalgam within us, this powerful spirit.

Imagine how strong you would be if you approached your work as a leader instinctively and intuitively, drawing from a wide range of dimensions from your palette. You may have taken a test that shows you as a Thinker—logical, reasonable, questioning, critical and tough—but as a leader in his or her full power, when circumstances require it, you are able to fully access your Feeler dimensions: empathetic, compassionate, accommodating, tender and accepting. Possibilities give you power. Forge ahead and load your brush with these colors on your palette as you need them, tapping into your full potential.

Great leaders not only draw much of their power by embracing who they really are—their strengths and weaknesses—they also recognize that all of it is important because it constitutes their authentic self. There is no power greater than the freedom and stability of operating from an authentic platform, comfortable with who we are. There is no template for the weakness-proof, perfect leader. Leaders come in all shapes and forms. Peter F. Drucker put it best: "Some of the best business and nonprofit CEOs I've worked with over a 65-year consulting career were not stereotypical leaders. They were all over the map in terms of their personalities, attitudes, values, strengths, and weaknesses."

When we choose to lead, we need to have the confidence to step out of the crowd—we need to have the agility to handle whatever comes our way. We encourage you to become an expert on your strengths, to confront yourself daily with them. Don't view their light through a keyhole; let them shine fully on those you lead.

LEADERSHIP EXPLORATIONS

A Gifted Leader: The Power of Valuing Your Strengths

Look back through your entire life and identify four times when you were at your best:

_____

_____

_____

_____

_____

_____

For each event, circle three talents from the list below that you relied upon, or were instrumental in helping you to be at your best.

Analysis	Evaluation	Opportunistic
Appreciation	Excellence	Optimism
Artistic	Execution	Persuasion
Challenging	Exploration	Problem-solving
Community	Expressive	Philosophy
Communication	Futuristic	Piloting
Competition	Focus	Possibilities
Conducting	Inspiration	Purpose
Connection	Intuition	Relating
Coordination	Inventiveness	Resourceful
Creativity	Investigation	Synthesis
Curiosity	Ideation	System-minded
Decision-making	Imagination	Teaching
Design	Implementation	Theories
Discipline	Ingenuity	Vision
Empathy	Judgment	Writer
Encouragement	Logic	

CHAPTER SIX

Harnessing Anger and Joy

The Power of Emotions

"Being able to enter flow is emotional intelligence at its best; flow represents perhaps the ultimate in harnessing the emotions in the service of performance and learning. In flow the emotions are not just contained and channeled, but positive, energized, and aligned with the task at hand."

DANIEL GOLEMAN

Emotion is defined in most dictionaries as a mental state or a rapid-response feeling that arises spontaneously rather than through a conscious effort. A narrow interpretation of this definition would suggest that emotions are totally beyond our control. In fact we do have considerable power: the power to be intentional about our use of emotion, to decide when to let an emotion flow unrestrained, and when to re-channel its course. There are three things that are important to know about emotions: emotions are about things that matter to us; they provide us with very useful information; and, the drive to

59

experience or not experience an emotion determines a lot of our behavior. This makes emotions one of the most powerful forces within us. As such, they are an essential component of our leadership portrait—a primary color on our palette.

Emotions can be a close ally or a strong opponent, depending on how conscious you are of their triggers, habitual manifestations and impact. They are portals of self-discovery if we choose to make them so. Nowhere does the adage that "knowledge is power" apply more aptly than in the case of knowledge of one's emotions.

Emotions are frequently referred to as energy in motion. This is an apt description, since one of the formal definitions of energy is "the potential for causing changes" and emotions definitely precipitate significant changes in our behavior. To get a sense of the power of emotions, think of the emotions that spur terrorism and war, on the one hand, and heroic acts of bravery or major movements in art, on the other hand. On a physical level, think about how the emotion of fear can bring about physiological changes such as a pounding heart, or how anger can constrict our vocal chords, how embarrassment makes us blush and how gratitude can make our face break into a smile. All of these changes are different forms of energy with different effects, positive or negative.

Yet the emphasis on rationality and order in our workplaces tend to marginalize and devalue emotions. This is an important aspect of leadership as it requires an extensive amount of energy to keep emotions in check. Conversely, the more we acknowledge and honor our emotions, expressing them authentically and intelligently, the more power we have to lead. Imagine yourself as a leader who readily displays potent emotional states such as intense enthusiasm, keen interest, unbridled curiosity, sheer exuberance, victory, great passion, joy, hope, optimism, pride, and gratitude. Surely these are what Bertrand Russell must have had in mind when he talked of "creative emotions from which a good life springs." Think about how potent these states make us feel: how energized we are in their grip; how we are filled with possibility when we experience them. Think of athletes who achieve excellence in their sport—consider the fervency, excitement, and intensity that they experience; their unwavering optimism and anticipation of winning. Could athletes perform at their best, devoid of emotion? So it is with leaders.

But what about the so-called "negative emotions"? Conventional wisdom would dictate that these need to be controlled or even shunned; however, we cannot select which emotions we will experience just as one would select a new shirt. Negative emotions are a natural part of who we are; they are a part of our emotional framework. While most of us aim to be in a positive state of mind all the time, the reality is that negative emotions encroach upon us whether we like it or not. The aim here, then, is to move away from the dichotomy positive/negative and to view all emotions as part of our overall emotional make-up—to accept the negative emotions without personal recrimination and to view them instead as messengers, carriers of important information about ourselves, imparting precious, personal data that can either fuel our power or rob us of it, like energy bandits. And the difference is in what we do with the information embedded in the emotions. Negative emotions are simply a signal to us that there is something that we are not able to handle in the moment. If we ignore the message, we start an energy leak. If, however, we take the time to become aware of what we are feeling, in the moment, and acknowledge the emotion, we are then able to use that intelligence to effectively deal with whatever is causing the negative emotion.

People who have learned to function in their power, those who are highly attuned self-scientists, have trained themselves to address the small droplets before they become a flood. Examples of emotions considered negative include fear, anger, envy, greed, and jealousy. Everyone experiences these primordial emotions, at one time or other, but people who function in their power, who are emotionally competent, embrace these as inevitable learning opportunities and are not immobilized by them. Just like in the third law of thermo dynamics where heat seeks out cold, these individuals have learned, through experience, that the largest supply of energy will be diverted to the negative emotions if we let it, depleting the fuel needed for higher thoughts and higher states of emotions. Instead, they will identify the true cause of these emotions and resolve to address the source rather than let the emotions carry the day.

This takes us to another key point. We need to be able to have access to the full range of our emotions. This gives us the opportunity to play with a full deck of cards. It makes us nimble and flexible enough to react to widely varied situations, and to adapt as necessary, to different environments. Emotions color and enrich our interactions and experiences. If we have a limited range of emotions that we draw upon, we end up with a lot less coloring. For example, reining in love and joy can also block empathy and compassion. And the same wall we build to keep negative emotions out can also prevent positive emotions from entering. Think about how much we would miss if we didn't experience some of these emotional states, for example: boldness, elation, respect, delight, dynamism, passion, remorse, impatience, sadness, and being appalled? Like an accomplished artisan, we need the full range of tools to function at our highest power, remembering that all emotions propel to action, even negative ones.

In addition to having access to the full repertoire of emotions, we also need to be intelligent about our emotions. So what does this mean? It means first of all being aware when the emotion surfaces and being able to correctly identify the emotion because it's difficult to react properly to an emotion that we can't describe. There are hundreds of emotions but most people can name less than a couple of dozen. While we all understand the primary emotions such as joy, sadness, anger and fear, many of us lack the emotional literacy to correctly identify the secondary ones, the low-powered ones such as being mildly hurt or upset, feeling somewhat tense or worried, dealing with vague doubts and undefined confusions, being slightly skeptical and a little overwhelmed, feeling non-specific franticness and unexplained stress or anxiety. And yet, most of us live in that terrain, it seems, for at least some part of our leadership careers. It is these minor emotional states that most often are our biggest energy drains, the culprits that can derail us from the achievement of our goals. Vincent Van Gogh referred to little emotions as "the great captains of our lives, and we obey them without realizing it." It behooves us to raise our self-awareness of the minor emotions and develop an action plan to understand their sources and to deal with them.

Being intelligent about our emotions also means being aware of the subtle nuances of various emotions. Armed with that information we can make appropriate behavioral decisions. For example, anger can have many flavors: it can be bitterness, resentment, or dislike, to name a few. Narrowing down which one it is goes a long way toward being able to understand the reasons behind the emotions and making intelligent decisions about how to respond to the situation so that we don't drain our power. So it is with joy as well. For instance, as we contemplate our eagerness to adopt a certain path, it is good to know whether the glowing feeling propelling us to action is just the excitement of the new, or a genuine thrill stemming from the tangible and real benefits that can come from the new path we are undertaking. This can add valuable information to our decision-making processes.

In our exploration of emotions, we also need to be cognizant that the manifestation of one emotion can also be a powerful clue to us about the absence of another emotion or state, since emotions tend to work in polarities. For example, an easy access to frustration or anger on daily issues can signal an absence of compassion. Feeling bored can be a sign of not being engrossed in what we do. Feeling discouraged alerts us to the fact that we are not inspired. Being envious can be a signal that we lack self-confidence. We can use the awareness of these emotions as tools to discover what simmers beneath the surface of these intense feelings.

Finally, even the most phlegmatic among us have emotional hot buttons—once pressed, these trigger automatic reactions that can rob us of our self-control and leadership power. Those who have very young children know exactly what we mean. Your children are experts at pressing the buttons because they know exactly where they are. They put them there. Who are the corporate button-pushers in your life? Following are some questions that are designed to provide you with a brief emotions check-up.

- Emotions are our behavioral signature. What do yours say?
- Are there some emotional patterns that you have fallen into? What insights do these give you?
- Can you pinpoint which issues are driving your emotions most of the time?
- If you were to map your emotions with certain individuals, what patterns emerge? Are there situations that consistently elicit

automatic emotional reactions? Do these serve you well? If not, what can you do?

- What or who unleashes your anger? How does defensive anger limit you?
- If you fear change, what is this emotion preventing you from doing?
- What are your emotional hot-buttons? Who presses them?
- Are you living in a bubble-wrap when it comes to emotions? Are there some emotions that you need to reclaim in your life? Are there particular situations where you might find yourself emotionally numb? What causes this?
- Language is a powerful emotional motivator. What do you say to yourself when you are alone? Do you inspire yourself? If you had to articulate this silent dialogue out loud in front of others, would it seem harsh in the light of day?
- How rich is your emotional vocabulary?
- How can you harness the passionate potential of your emotions?
- Which emotions drain you of your energy on a regular basis? What can you do about it? How can you use awareness of your emotions, in the moment, to shift your energy if you need to?

There is an exhilarating feeling when you are in charge of yourself. Having an understanding of the role that emotions play in your life as a leader is an important part of this take charge process. So, how are emotions manifested in your leadership portrait? Are you pleased with the intensity of their color? Are there any emotions conspicuously absent from your palette? We encourage you to make the connection between your emotions and your power to lead: Understanding how emotions actively influence your reactions and experiences as a leader and how emotions are a powerful way by which we evaluate situations and make decisions. Consider embarking on a self-reflective journey of how you can harness the power of emotions to create what you want, and how you can, through awareness of your inner landscape, channel your emotions as a source of energy and creativity rather than derailment. Your emotions, like a mirror, reflect your thinking. What image do you see in the mirror?

LEADERSHIP EXPLORATIONS

Harnessing Anger and Joy: The Power of Emotions

Emotional Self-Awareness

Think about your emotional world as having an inner and an outer dimension. Your inner dimension is the part of you that is very private and may not be readily exposed to others. Your outer dimension is that part of you that others see and with which they interact on a regular basis. Now consider these two dimensions to be separated by a barrier, and each side of the barrier is engraved with a list of your most prevalent emotions.

The following list contains words that are often used to describe an emotional or mental state. From this list, select the words that depict your most prevalent emotions or mental states and write these words on the appropriate side of the barrier, i.e., inner or outer.

Content	Cold	Strong
Frightened	Important	Kind
Safe	Sad	Bold
Joyful	Warm	Courageous
Helpless	Apprehensive	Excited
Repressed	Glad	Happy
Tired	Bad	Virtuous
Hurt	Weak	Helpful
Cynical	Brave	Proud
Miserable	Generous	Rejected
Optimistic	Pessimistic	Satisfied
Serious	Unhappy	Indifferent
Connected	Disrespectful	

Do your inner and outer dimensions reflect the same reality or is there a significant disconnection between what you show on the outside and what you experience on the inside? When you visualize your barrier, do you see it as impenetrable or porous? Do you readily allow deeply held emotions to surface and be incorporated into your interactions with others? Are you able to manage your visible emotions and pull them behind your barrier when appropriate? Do your emotions provide you power in your interactions with others or are they unmanaged hindrances?

As you reflect on your inner and outer emotional dimensions, what are the implications for you as a leader?

_____

_____

_____

_____

_____

_____

_____

_____

_____

_____

When we get "hooked," our most negative emotions are brought, involuntarily, into the interaction. Identify five statements or actions that others make that most frequently "hook" you.

Emotion   **"Hook" Statement or Action**

_____   _____

_____   _____

_____   _____

_____   _____

_____   _____

_____   _____

_____   _____

What are the implications of being "hooked" by these statements on your ability to lead?

_____

_____

_____

_____

_____

_____

_____

_____

_____

_____

_____

In what ways do you "hook" others?

Name   **Statement or Action**

_____   _____

_____   _____

_____   _____

_____   _____

_____   _____

_____   _____

_____   _____

_____   _____

_____   _____

_____   _____

_____   _____

_____   _____

_____   _____

_____   _____

CHAPTER SEVEN

It's Not About You

The Power of Humility

"We come nearest to the great when we are great in humility."

R. TAGORE

When you read the biographies of the great leaders in history, two themes are often interwoven through the pages: a gratitude for the opportunity to serve others, and humility in the face of the challenges of leadership. We gain true and lasting power when we realize that, even though leaders are often in the spotlight, true leadership is about others, not about us. When we shed pretense and false pride, when we act from a lack of self-importance, and, in short, when we practice the simple art of being humble, we lead. Humility, sometimes confused with self-abasement, is in fact, totally the contrary. Humility elevates us and gives us power in many ways. Consider the amount of energy that we waste to keep our masks in place—the public disguises we wear to hide the fact that we are imperfect. The great leader recognizes that no matter what levels we have achieved, we are not always right, we cannot have all the answers and we do make mistakes. People see behind the masks and yet we often expend a great deal of energy on our masks, on keeping up the image that we are infallible. Imagine the amount of time and energy that is suddenly freed when we decide to embrace our humanness, when we decide to be genuine.

Consider, as well, the fact that people we seek to lead are attracted to those who display qualities of genuine humility and, conversely, are repelled by arrogance, hubris, and excessive pride. These cause negative responses in others and constitute another energy drain as we try to manage the consequences of these reactions.

It is not an easy endeavor to consistently practice humility when you are blessed with being in a position of authority and enjoying all of the executive perks and all of the trappings of leadership success. We need to remember that having an office with a door, or a chauffeur and private plane, or a title of "shift supervisor" are all trappings of office that can be transient. What is not transient is the impact we have on people. As managers, we work with business models, with systems and processes–this is what we manage. But as leaders, it is people that we lead, not systems or processes. The power associated with being a leader can make us forget this privilege. If we stop to think for a minute what that privilege entails, we would be in awe of our role in leading people. This responsibility should humble us. Leadership is a calling–leading people, having an impact on their careers and lives, is a special advantage and should be treated as such. When we view it this way, when we consider it a privilege to lead people, this attitude becomes ingrained in our daily routines, and people respond positively to this. When we are grateful to have the opportunity to lead, others sense this and allow us significant leeway.

How humbling, and at the same time ennobling, it is to approach our leadership from the point of view of what we can do for others rather than what we can do for ourselves. Much has been said about servant leadership but it bears repeating. As Robert Greenleaf aptly put it long ago: "… it begins with the natural feeling that one wants to serve, to serve first." When we focus on growing those we lead, we grow ourselves. When we focus on giving power to those we lead, we gain even greater power.

One thing to remember is that we lead at pleasure of the people within our organizations. At any time, we can lose their support and thereby our leadership. As with beauty, leadership is in the eye of the beholder. All of this should be a humbling perspective. The leadership arena is rife with stories of egocentric leaders who have hastened their demise because of their arrogance. People go the extra mile to support an unassuming leader who treats them with respect and dignity and, conversely, withhold their discretionary effort from the arrogant, self-important leader. Any time people withhold their best from us, we are weakened. We lose.

In your dealings with those you lead, is there room enough for them in every encounter? Or is the entire space occupied by you? People want to see the bigger version of them reflected back in their leader's eyes; this precious image will not be there if we are self-important. With an arrogant leader, there is room only for their small self, not their big self. How do people feel about themselves when they are in your presence? We cannot set out to make everyone like us. We cannot control how people feel about us. But we can work on how people feel about themselves when they are in our presence. This is the discipline of selfless leadership.

So what is the profile of a leader who practices genuine humility? First, such leaders are comfortable with their own stories: whether it is about good or bad times, whether it is times when they were up or times when they were down. They are comfortable in their own skin—comfortable with who they are. Second, they are very open about their need for ongoing leadership development. They see their need to develop as leaders like everyone else. Third, they constantly seek peer-to-peer communication. When you are in their presence, they see themselves as equal in humanity. And that is a powerful quality.

LEADERSHIP EXPLORATIONS
It's Not About You: The Power of Humility

To whom are you most indebted for your success? List their names below and note how they helped you succeed.

1. _____
   _____
   _____
   _____

2. _____
   _____
   _____
   _____

3. _____
   _____
   _____
   _____

4. _____
   _____
   _____
   _____

5. _____
   _____
   _____
   _____

6. _____
   _____
   _____
   _____

As you reflect on the ways others have helped you, what shift in your attitude might you need to make to see your leadership as primarily a role of servanthood?

_____

_____

_____

_____

_____

_____

_____

Select three junior individuals with whom you interact on a regular basis. Add their names and a brief description of their roles in your organization. What perspectives or opinions of these individuals do you need to change in order for you to see them as people to be served?

Name	Name	Name

_____

_____

_____

_____

_____

_____

_____

_____

_____

_____

_____

_____

INTERVIEW

It's Not About You: The Power of Humility

Marsha Royer
Vice President, Human Resources
Schweitzer Engineering Laboratories Inc.

I have always learned most from being an observer. I can't recall exactly when it was, in my observations, that I discovered the importance of humility. I remember one individual in particular who clearly modeled it. I had ample opportunities to observe his behavior as one of his staff members. He was a man with an imposing presence that carried significant power. I watched him move almost invisibly sometimes, catlike, through the clutter that frequently exists in corporate life. He didn't speak to power. He simply had it, and trusted it. He had the humility to seek council, he trusted himself to make wise decisions, to examine the data necessary to ensure the business moved steadily forward. Everyone in the team respected him and showed him obvious affection. His leadership ability was never questioned. He was incredibly 'present' wherever he was. I found that intriguing. I watched him in meetings, sitting quietly and then calmly making powerful, cogent observations. People around him listened.

At that time, I was just beginning to learn about power in the corporate world. I was still fragile in my own sense of self, particularly about my judgment in business matters. His modeling brought me to the understanding that trusting myself, and, above all, being authentic, is a source of great power. It's what gave me the opportunity to lead wonderful teams of people by accepting that I am always listening, learning, growing—knowing that making a mistake, apologizing, or not fighting when it may have been expected, have resulted in my building a quiet power to make changes that I could have only dreamed of had I followed other leaders' models. Those models of telling, not asking; driving others for the sake of personal advancement; throwing positional weight around for show; demanding respect, always being right—we have all seen those. Many of those models quickly flame out or manage to knock themselves out of the competition for the most coveted leadership roles. These individuals are often noisy, uncomfortable, phantom power holders and unfortunate shooting stars. And even when they aren't shooting stars, they are not much cared for by the people around them.

Over the years, building trust in my own judgment has been strengthened by watching people who work for me become successful and make positive changes in their own environments. If I were ever to bask in my personal power, it would be on those occasions when a change has been made for the better and no one knows for sure how that happened. I take great glee in 'being a mole'—in planting the seed of an idea, nurturing it and watching it take root and grow into a positive change for people, employees, customers, the business itself. I have been graced with listening to employees discuss how things have been changing for the better; or how we made such a great decision on a particular business venture, or employee program ... without anyone knowing exactly what had occurred. Even better than that is listening to them speak to the role they had in making it happen, watching them grow. Planting seeds and stepping back—one of my daughters has a signature line on her e-mail that says: "True success is planting trees under which you will never sit." I have to smile at that, both because of the thought, and the quiet pride I take in knowing her heart came to that thought by seeds that I may have helped to plant in her vision of the world.

I am convinced that true leaders don't talk about power. They don't have to. They touch the world and positively change it by how they live in the world. They model the way they wish the world to be. Mahatma Gandhi said: "We must be the change we wish to see in this world." My experience is tied directly to that, and I am frequently amazed by how powerful any person's life can be when they live authentically, with heart. The concept of high self-esteem is, to me, a residual effect of believing in and trusting oneself. Actually, esteem is not about self at all, but about the way others trust you, and know they can rely on you to be honest and caring in all your dealings with them.

Humility is simply knowing who you are and loving the place you hold in the world. On days when I am particularly challenged or am not feeling as centered as I would like to be, stopping to look at how the people on the team are doing, how they are growing, is direct reassurance that my contribution is real. Watching and knowing that every person I touch in turn touches someone else, carries tremendous responsibility for me. I believe if I model that encounter with heart and positive effort, the simple power of that will keep flowing from that person on to others they touch. When we respect each encounter, it results in a personal sense of confidence and gentle power. For me, not desiring power, but searching to do 'the right thing', is what ultimately results in true power. And true power never needs to be flexed—it simply is.

CHAPTER EIGHT

Decisions, Decisions, Decisions

The Power of Choice

"The greatest power that a person possesses is the power to choose."

J. MARTIN KOHE

Every day we have a choice in how we show up on our leadership path. The ability to choose is an extraordinary source of power that often remains untapped. Great artists develop unique and inventive ways of manipulating pigment. You can, too, when you paint your leadership portrait–by making a deliberate choice to increase the range of talents that you use, attitudes that you display, or emotions that you access in your daily repertoire. These are what we consider the range of colors and hues on your palette–in using this wide array of possibilities, you add brilliance and rich complexity to your leadership portrait. Imagine that you wake up in the morning and decide what attitude to adopt, what talents to use, what strengths to draw upon, what to pay attention to, what to ignore, where to channel your thoughts, how to manage your feelings and what personal actions to take. Imagine how powerful you would be, knowing that this is all within your reach. The tools to accomplish this are all within your control. Your choices determine the core essence of who you are. "One's philosophy," said Eleanor Roosevelt, "is not best expressed in words; it is expressed in the choices one makes." However, if you only choose what you think is reasonable or possible, you short-change yourself. It is by aiming for the highest targets that we arrive at greatness. What choices are you going to make today to enrich your palette, to access the infinity of possibilities?

We all carry within us a mental model of who we are. But all models are a simplification of reality, intended to turn the complex into the simple. We are infinitely more complex and vast, more filled with a possibility of being than our mental models can possibly ever represent. The model of ourselves that we carry in our minds is in fact a straight-jacket, one that shapes our perceptions of ourselves and limits us; it places invisible, yet impenetrable, boundaries on what we think we can do, on what talents we use, on what powers we have.

We can move out of the confines of our mental models through awareness and self-determination. Take for example your decision-making style. You may be pre-wired to adopt one style that you feel at ease with, such as a predilection to seek complete consensus before you proceed. You can expand from that and choose any style that works best for you in the moment. So, notwithstanding your view of yourself as an inclusive collaborator, when there are situations that call for a fiercely independent approach, you can simply decide that this is the approach that you will adopt. This is the power of your palette–the power of challenging your thinking patterns and behavioral habits that restrict you. It's the power to break free from the shackles of stasis and boundaries.

John Gardner said: "Most human talent remains undeveloped." We challenge you to undertake a discovery journey to look in all the corners of your intellect and your heart to uncover every talent you are gifted with that is untapped. What are some of your raw talents that have been undeveloped? What do you have to do to bring these to the fore? What talents have you not expressed lately? What under-used skills have not been enhanced and nurtured? What are some of the blockages that need to be cleared for you to utilize these talents? Just as combinations of primary colors create secondary colors, what minor talents do you have that, by their combination, become a powerful tool for you? What talents do you hold in exile? What can you do to bring them back? How can you make use of them in your current role? Are some of these talents intentionally quarantined? What circumstances led to this? Are these circumstances still valid? How would this enhance your personal power? You increase your palette by becoming aware of these hidden, undeveloped, unexpressed and banished talents, and adding them as extra hues on your leadership palette. We encourage you not to leave the use of your talents to chance and to be deliberate about them, to use them all to illuminate your role as a leader.

Another way to increase your palette is also by focusing on what needs to be eliminated. An artist dips his paintbrush in a glass of water to remove a color; what is in your palette that you need to remove? What thoughts, attitudes or emotions darken your portrait? Just as our choice of action is important, so is our choice of attention. You have tremendous power when you consciously decide what you will no longer focus your attention on, what doesn't serve to propel you forward in your leadership quest. Some opportunities for leadership power are airborne. They occur when we are focused, when we live in the moment. Could some of these be passing by unnoticed as you focus elsewhere? What is your internal focus of attention, that which occupies the biggest real estate in your mental space? Does it serve you well?

As leaders, we constantly make and unmake ourselves. What new approaches can you take to throw the doors wide open to the way you see yourself? What assumptions do you need to shed? Do you see yourself as having choices in every aspect of your leadership behavior? For example, if you see yourself as a "thinker," an analytical individual, always identifying what is wrong so that you can problem-solve, you can choose to dip your brush into the "feeler" part of your palette and practice appreciation and support, and look for qualities to praise. If you have labeled yourself as a "sensor," practical, factual and concrete, handling conflict with opinions and principles, you can choose to step out of that circle and focus on the imaginative, the abstract and theoretical, and handle conflict with needs and values. Are you a detailed individual? Why not decide to focus on patterns of ideas as well? Do you focus on the past and present? How about asking what could be? Are you jazzed by the joy of closure? How about the joy of the process? What would be the impact of including both dimensions in your power to lead? Would it make you more effective, versatile, and present in the moment? How about your learning style—do you like to follow instructions? How about making up your own directions sometimes? Do you trust material as it is imparted? What about delving between the lines?

Think about the lens you may be using to view yourself that may distort the image that you see. As Mark Twain might have said: "Is your imagination out of focus?" Face the image you see squarely, challenge it, and compare it to a more sophisticated ideal. What do you see? What current circumstances or mind-set are causing the gap?

Benjamin Zander said: "You can turn your attention away from the onslaught of circumstances and listen for the music of your being." What music do you choose to play? Where are your choices leading you? Is it where you want to go? Viewing everything about you through the lens of possibility, being wide open, is a powerful tool in your arsenal as a leader. We encourage you to make the power of choice a daily habit and a key part of your approach to leadership. There are two ways artists paint—with broad and easy strokes, or with narrow and hard ones. Which one will you choose when you paint your leadership portrait?

LEADERSHIP EXPLORATIONS

Decisions, Decisions, Decisions: The Power of Choice

Consider the following major areas of your life and determine:

a. The extent to which you or others are making the decisions that impact these areas

b. The quality of decisions made in this area in the past 12 months

Aspect	% Decisions: Me	% Decisions: Others	Decision Quality
Work Schedule			
Personal Schedule			
Business Plans: Strategic Imperatives			
Attire			
Leisure Pursuits			
Personal Development			
Health and Fitness			
Relationships			
Financial Matters			
Priorities			

In which three areas of your life, would higher quality deci
sions have the most positive influence on you and your world?

1. _____

_____

2. _____

_____

3. _____

_____

Decision-Making Habits

Identify immediate opportunities to make high-quality decisions
in each of these areas each day in the coming week:

	M	T	W	T	F	S	S
1.							
2.							
3.							

Your Future

Think of the issues you worry about in your personal and professional life. Are they important and controllable? Are they important but not controllable? Are they unimportant and controllable? Or, are they unimportant and not controllable?

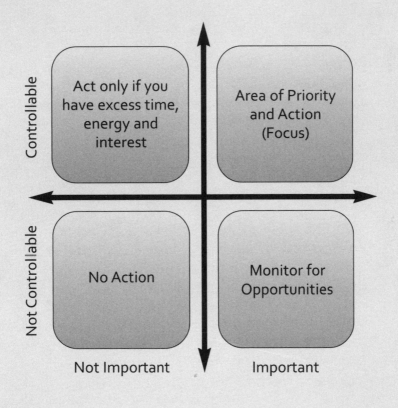

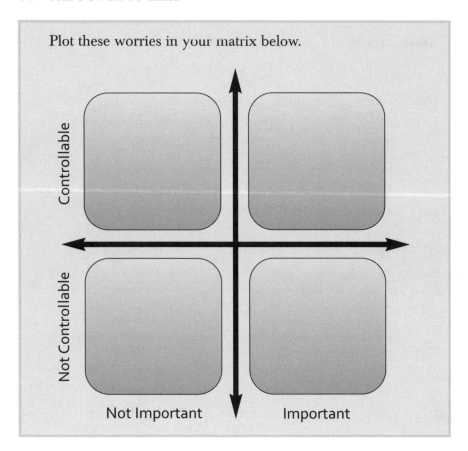

INTERVIEW

Decisions, Decisions, Decisions: The Power of Choice

Karin Kirkpatrick, MBA, CHRP, CPC
Director, Centre for CEO Leadership, Sauder School of Business
The University of British Columbia

My decision-making style has changed over the years. I used to be quite quick to arrive at decisions—relying strongly on my gut feeling and instinct. This worked for me sometimes, but often, it resulted in an emotional, rather than a practical solution. I find that decision-making is a learned art and an important one for leaders.

Choosing the path of least resistance is not a part of my style of leadership. I have always felt a strong desire to push to the next level, to redefine my idea of success as achieving more than I have currently achieved. I would call this my unconscious decision making—simply the way that I am wired. As my self-awareness became stronger, I came to the realization that this is the kind of decision making process that I needed to watch for. I believe that strong self-awareness is key to effective leadership and self-management. As I evolve as a person and as a leader, I am better able to balance my choices. First I decide what feels right, as instinct will always still play a role in my choices. But then I take it further. I picture myself in the future having made each of the choices. How did the choice impact me? How did it impact others in my team? What are the possible outcomes? Which road today will lead to the place I most want to be?

One of the big changes in the way I make decisions is I now canvas others in my team and seek feedback on my choices. In the past, decision making for me had always been a solitary activity. I now find it very useful and clarifying to have trusted others to reflect my thoughts back to me through their own lens and perspective. This provides immense value.

As a leader, the ability to make decisions is the attribute which most demonstrates to followers that you have the power and confidence to lead.

Indecisive leaders do not have the confidence of their teams. I have witnessed this in successful leaders, and I experienced it myself in leading my own company several years ago.

I would like to share what is probably the most important decision I made in my life. It wasn't the choice to start my business, nor to go back to school to earn several degrees, nor to start a family. It was simply the choice to start choosing. I literally had an epiphany in my mid-twenties that changed the course of my life. This was a particularly difficult period in my life, with many false starts, detours that led nowhere and the prospect of not achieving my dreams. I woke up that day, looking around me and had total clarity: I came to the realization that there was no one to blame for my status quo—we are all, in large part, responsible for our destiny. At that moment, I realized that I had the power to change everything. I really could do whatever I wanted. I still remember the euphoria I felt at that moment, and even now, years later, I can recall that experience as vividly as if it happened yesterday. And any time during stressful and difficult events, when I feel an inclination to place the blame on circumstances or others, I think about that day. That was the day I made the choice to choose the course that my life was to take. I owe my success to that simple yet powerful shift in my mindset. The power to choose is perhaps the most important power we have in our personal and our professional lives.

CHAPTER NINE

In Their Shoes

The Power of Empathy

"We experience ourselves, our thoughts and feelings as something separate from the rest. A kind of optical delusion of consciousness. This delusion is a kind of prison for us, restricting us to our personal desires and to affection for a few persons nearest to us. Our task must be to free ourselves from the prison by widening our circle of compassion to embrace all living creatures and the whole of nature in its beauty."

ALBERT EINSTEIN

Dictionaries often define empathy as feeling what others feel. Think about the implications of this for you as a leader. Can you really put yourself so deeply into the shoes of those you lead that you can actually experience their feelings? As articulated in Albert Einstein's quotation above, we often confine our attention solely to our personal concerns, and to the concerns of a few people who are close to us. This tendency holds us captive in a narrow enclave from which it is impossible to truly expand our power, our power to lead in a way that has substance and significance.

87

No matter how accomplished we are, no matter how many skills, talents and achievements we can claim as ours, no matter how wide our personal influence, it is all ultimately hollow if it does not include empathy for all those who surround us, for the people who do the work for our team, our unit or our organizations.

A formal definition of empathy is the ability to identify and understand another's situation, feelings, and motives. It's our capacity to recognize and vicariously experience the concerns and issues others are facing. The metaphor language for empathy includes putting yourself in the other person's shoes—or seeing things through someone else's eyes. Our First Nations people have a beautiful way of expressing empathy as "walking a mile in someone else's moccasins." Moccasins are a symbol of the strength of Native North American people. This gives an even more profound interpretation of empathy as the ability to understand the struggles and challenges others face and the fortitude it requires to endure these challenges and stay the course.

But we are not concerning ourselves here with the conventional interpretation of empathy—that is, with demonstrating an understanding of others' points of view or feelings. While this is a prime skill for any leader, what we want to focus on is another dimension of empathy, much deeper, more elemental, and infinitely more powerful in its positive effect on others—and the ricocheting effect it has on us and on our power to lead. It is about having a deeper connection with people who enter our lives; a genuine link moving from a surface association to a deeper person-to-person relationship.

So what does this relationship entail? It involves seeing people in a way that can only come from a genuine concern for their welfare and success—seeing them in ways that they may have not seen themselves. Picasso once said: "I see for others in order to put on canvas the sudden apparitions which come to me." The leader who has this deep seated empathy develops these kinds of eyes—eyes that move away from self-focus to focusing on the other and, in the moment, seeing the very best that is at the core of that person and reflecting it back to the individual. This leader sees the spirit of greatness, the vast potential that dwells in the person and is waiting to be released. It's seeing beyond our eyes, seeing past people's self-imposed limitations and barriers. It is peeling labels off people, and truly seeing our fellow humans. In so doing, it is discovering the promise and the spark in each person. It's seeing with our heart.

This type of empathy also means having a heightened awareness of when we begin to have stagnant impressions of people, impressions we formed based on a first meeting or on a past incident. It's ensuring that our opinion about a particular person is not fossilized, but, instead, continues to evolve to allow for subsequent positive impressions to alter original ones.

Empathy is also realizing that we are echoes of those around us, those through whom we accomplish so much in our leadership journey. It is not losing sight of how much of our success is dependent on other people's efforts, contributions and talents. As leaders, we are not only judged on what we do, but to a very large extent, on what we inspire others to do, on what we achieve through them. Empathy, then, is the understanding and honoring of the role others play and connecting our personal power to them, as a conduit for them to realize their own aspirations and dreams. It's having the willingness, and making the allowance of time, to look into people's hearts so as to glean what these aspirations are. It's truly feeling these aspirations and realizing that they are no less intense and no less important than our own aspirations. But it doesn't stop there. It's about opening the portals for the expression and realization of these aspirations; it's about providing the opportunities for people to realize their own potential for greatness. In *Creating the Good Life: Applying Aristotle's Wisdom to Find Meaning and Happiness,* James O'Toole talks about this worthy intention: "If Aristotle is right that the good life depends on developing one's human potential, then providing the conditions in which employees can do so is a clear moral responsibility of leaders of work organizations ... [Leaders who] deny employees the chance to develop their potential deny them the opportunity to develop their humanity."[4]

How do we help others realize their full potential? We do so by believing in them, in their potential for greatness; by helping them discover their gifts and expand their abilities; by challenging them and by acknowledging them for what they try to create of themselves. We also help them make the connection between who they are and the vision of who they can be. And we go out of our way to use our leadership power to make that vision come alive.

It's a de-centering of the self and developing a powerful antenna for others' lives, for understanding their actions, attitudes and their needs. It's being able to perceive what's important to the other person and to enter their experience. It's feeling a genuine interest for making the person feel valued. This particular manifestation of empathy for the people we lead enriches our capacity as leaders. It provides the light under which others are able to shine, while at the same time, it makes us stand out. It takes our leadership portrait from the grey twilight to the glowing richness of full color. This empathy manifestation is, in short, one of the noblest actions and most valuable we can undertake as leaders.

LEADERSHIP EXPLORATIONS

In Their Shoes: The Power of Empathy

Practicing Empathy

Select six people whom you know reasonably well and predict the following:

Name	Core Values	Biggest Aspirations	Personality	Fears	Sources of Happiness
1.					
2.					
3.					
4.					
5.					
6.					

Considering the above, how do you think each of these individuals sees you?

1. _____

_____

_____

2. _____

_____

_____

3. _____
_____
_____

4. _____
_____
_____

5. _____
_____
_____

6. _____
_____
_____

Select five key members in your organization. If you could grant each a wish, what do you think they would wish for?

Name   **Wish**

1. _____
_____

2. _____
_____

3. _____
_____

4. _____
_____

5. _____
_____

INTERVIEW

In Their Shoes: The Power of Empathy

Mike Szczechura
Vice President, Ad Sales, Charter Media®

I would like to share a story that I was fortunate enough to witness in my most recent position as the Vice President of Sales and Operations for Charter Media® in the St. Louis area. This was the classic case of the horn or halo effect. Being new to the company, and to the position, I immediately started my "inspection tour" of my new team. As is often the case, whether I asked for an assessment, or whether it was volunteered, people gave me their opinions of various members of the team. One individual, who is at the center of this story, was viewed negatively by others. I was told that she was hard to get along with, that she became argumentative and, was often, impatient with people. Her role was to monitor inventory, and to make sure that our sales people knew when there were areas of opportunity (i.e., continue to sell, we have plenty of inventory) or when to raise a red flag (i.e., this network or time-frame is dangerously close to sell out or is sold out). We met and had a chance to talk briefly; she seemed to me to be a pleasant enough person. I didn't give further thought about the negative comments I had received about her until I hired a new director of operations; she was to report to the new director. As he and I talked about expectations for his role, and what his plans were as he took on his new responsibilities, we discussed this individual as part of his team. I told him my experience with her, but also of the opinions about her that I heard from others. So, in essence, I was promulgating the horn effect around this individual because of the global impression others had of her. Maximizing the yield from our inventory is critical to success, delivering what we sell is paramount to the long term success of our business, and to our customers' business as well. This was exactly how this individual felt. She had passion. She wanted to be heard when she sounded the alarm. She knew she had something to contribute that was critical to our success. Was her behavior, as perceived by others, simply a manifestation of her frustration of not being heard? This was not to say that inventory management was not important to the company before, but because we elevated the importance of this aspect to the success of our business, and because our new director refused to take assessments of others as the only truth, there was an important shift in this individual. The director saw the passion and talent in the way she approached her job and made sure to let me know when she contributed, so that I, too, could acknowledge her—and this unleashed greater productivity on her part as she now knew that she was appreciated and valued and is an awesome member of our ever-improving team. Thanks to our Director, we peeled off the labels that were placed on this person and we were able to truly see with our heart rather than stop at the surface behavior.

It's important to me, as a leader, to connect with all the people who do the work in our teams. I communicate with people in different ways. When I am in the front of a room, speaking to a group of people, I watch for signals to see if I have connected. I try to have as many one-on-one, face-to-face conversations. I have found that this is when I have had the greatest connection to the other person. I have to work at this—in other words, I have to plan and make the time to have regular one-on-one meetings with my team members. Recently, we instituted a program whereby, once a month, groups of eight, from all departments of our company, meet with me for lunch. This is on a volunteer basis. It's an open forum format and I ask them for their thoughts regarding a variety of issues such as how are we doing, are we living our mission, are we engaged in our core values, and, if you owned the company or were placed in charge, what three things would you do. Not only do I feel a greater connection, but I am witnessing members of various departments starting to connect with each other during the 60–90 minutes we spend together. Some good ideas have emerged from these meetings, and those that are easily actionable, are implemented within a couple of days. I make sure to communicate that to the group. When you listen, you hear that people want to do their best; they're seeking validation and, when necessary, guidance. Often times, it's just a matter of asking people: "When will you do that?"

The open forum lunch is one way that allows me to stay connected to the various parts of the organization. The only time when I feel that I am standing apart as the leader and not included, is when I allow myself to be marginalized. My experience, in these occasions, is more about not being connected rather than not being included. Where I haven't made the effort, I inherently know that I am less connected. When I'm connected, it's because I have taken action to do so. So it is about being proactive and making the effort to find ways to connect with people. Provided you've hired well, most people are looking for ways to shine: Give them that gift, that opportunity to show you how great they are, based on where they are in their development. Look for ways for people to contribute to the team as a part of their development plan. People never forget this.

Make sure that you are connected enough to know when things are going right and take the opportunity to let people know of your acknowledgement and appreciation, but also have the courage not to engage in self-deception if you sense that things aren't quite right. Not making connections gives you plenty of time to engage in self-deception—don't let this happen. Making connections gets more people working on "what we want to be" in our organizations.

PART THREE

Your Masterpiece

CHAPTER TEN

Scrape Off Old Paint

The Power of Your Thoughts

"Self-reverence, self-knowledge, self-control—these three alone lead life to sovereign power."

ALFRED LORD TENNYSON

In artists' parlance, saturation refers to the purity of a color. A pure color is at its highest saturation—that is, it is at its brightest and most intense form. Artists decrease the intensity of a color by mixing white, black and other colors to a pure color. Just as artists weaken a color by mixing in other colors, so we too lose our own intensity and our own brilliance when we clutter our minds with irrelevant and adverse thinking. Leadership requires a single-mindedness that can only be achieved when we de-junk our minds of undisciplined thinking habits and erroneous assumptions. A wealth of personal power is at our disposal when we decide to exercise control over the quality of our thoughts, when we take control of our mind, that is, when we start to think about our own thinking. Ekhart Tolle in *The Power of Now* calls this "watching the thinker," which is another way of saying listen to the voice in your head—be there as the witnessing presence.[5]

What does this process entail? It starts with self-examination—that is, intentionally monitoring our thoughts and reactions to our

99

experiences. We need to acknowledge first that we cannot control all the thoughts that come into our mind uninvited, but what we can do, is decide to raise our awareness of our thoughts so that we can become conscious of what is happening in our mental world. What are your habitual thoughts? Are they thoughts that advance your dreams? Or are they thoughts that drain your mental energy? What about habitual thoughts that you have regarding your leadership? Effective leaders are continually reevaluating and upgrading their thoughts on leadership. Are you doing the same? Have you updated your views of leadership to reflect your current position or situation or are you leading with precepts acquired long ago? For example, if you believed that a leader sets the vision and inspires others to follow, is this still a reality that reflects your current leadership environment? If not, have you given some thought to what exactly that reality is? For example, is the vision based on the collective imagination of your organization's members? If this is the case, the outdated notion falls in the category of mind junk that prevents you from achieving clarity and thereby minimizes your personal power.

And what about habitual thoughts and assumptions you may have regarding the people in your work life? Do you view your young constituents differently than you view the older ones? How so? Do you tend to view employees who work longer hours more favorably than those who value work/family balance? Do you tend to have more trust for those who communicate more frequently with you? Do you have defined views of female vs. male leadership styles? How do you rate the risk takers amongst your constituents vs. those who adopt a more cautious approach? Do you instinctively react differently to extraverts than introverts? Do you believe that innovative members of your team have a natural talent that others cannot learn or acquire? What are your thoughts regarding those in your team who challenge others in relation to those who promote harmony? What about those who habitually challenge you? When we examine these and other such views, under a reality lens, we need to ask ourselves, if our views stand up to the test of scrutiny. Do these views help us or hinder us? And how might these hindering views be palpable to others—that is, when we are in the presence of these people, are we behaving in a set way, driven by our habitual thoughts about them? What is the effect of that on our personal leadership? Are there repercussions that we might not have been aware of, subtle repercussions that erode our power to lead? Finally, we encourage you to ponder how these views might prevent you from growing to your fullest potential as a leader. What can you do today to revamp your thoughts about the people you work with in order to help them achieve greatness? How can helping them achieve greatness enhance your own greatness?

Apart from our habitual thoughts on leadership and our engrained thoughts about the people with whom we work, we all have compulsive thoughts that enter our mind on a consistent basis. Without going into the well-researched psychological principles involved, it can be reasonably assumed that we are carrying some thought patterns and assumptions that have been ingrained in us since childhood. These thoughts may not always serve us well in our leadership roles. Now may be a good time to examine your entire thinking process. Once we have taken inventory of the recurrent themes in our mental life, we are then better able to recognize and purge the unhelpful intruders. There are many benefits to training ourselves to be aware and minimize the effect that habitual, unconscious, unproductive thoughts have on us. For example, we are not trapped by these thoughts—by releasing the hold that such thoughts have on us, on our behavior, we are better able to focus on what we really want to do. Recognizing the nature of these thoughts and stopping them the instant we become aware of them frees up our attention for more affirming thoughts that enhance our leadership effectiveness.

There are also habitual thoughts that are not necessarily negative, but that we may have outgrown. They may have been a part of our ethos early in our career, but they are no longer applicable to a leader's life. Like an object we may have bought decades ago which is now no longer in favor due to our changing taste or economic status, so it is with some habitual, ingrained thoughts.

Apart from habitual thoughts, there is also what we call "junk thoughts." Junk thoughts come in two forms: The first, like junk

objects, are simply not useful. They have no value. In this category
we can include thoughts of regret, or dwelling on thoughts of past
conversations, or obsessing over events over which we have no control. The second type of junk thought, and probably the one that constitutes the biggest obstacle, is emotional. It is often a recurrent
thought of personal criticism which has been directed at us and
which we carry around with us. It can pop up like a jack-in-the-box,
unexpected. It can often surface by association—that is, a particular
experience will remind us of it and once we are reminded, we
indulge in the thought, see it to fruition and then re-experience the
associated emotions. Other such thoughts relate to fear of what is
unknown, worry over possible future events or perceived or imag-
ined slights. They involve entertaining thoughts of anger, nurturing
thoughts of self-doubt instead of tossing them out, revisiting misun-
derstandings and dwelling on past annoyances. Once awareness sets
in, we can consciously choose to let go of these types of emotional
junk thoughts. Choice gives us power.

That power is nowhere more crucial than when we consider the
most insidious form of emotional mind-clutter, the clutter that comes
from not enjoying who you are as a person. If this is the case, we
encourage you to consider what it is that you might not like about
yourself and develop a blueprint of what you need to do to simply be
the person that you would like to be. To that end, consider borrow-
ing from others' palettes—let the wisdom and ethos of those you
admire be your inspirational guide.

And what about the mind-junk that results from what has been
called cognitive dissonance in psychology.[6] Cognitive dissonance is
the awareness of inconsistencies between our beliefs and our actions
which result in conflicting states of mind. For example, we may
strongly believe we have a carefully thought out strategy for a new
and exciting business idea, but it stays for years as an unrealized
vision because we never have the confidence to take some steps to
test it or to put it into action. Thoughts of it intrude into our mind,
every now and then, but it continues to stay as just that: thoughts that
intrude. If we don't take any action, then the thoughts over the years
are merely junk items, much like objects that occupy physical space

but have not been used for years. This type of mind-junk is perhaps one of the most detrimental to us as it rarely enters our consciousness without leaving a residue of anxiety at the unfulfilled potential. Along those lines, unfinished business can also constitute mind junk as it drains us every time we think of it. So indecision is also a form of mind clutter.

Let us also not forget the clutter generated by some forms of communication—not only what we say to ourselves, but also what we say to others. What proportion of your communication is important or significant as opposed to merely surface or even trivial? How much mental bandwidth is unnecessarily used up in overcomplicating our communication, by using circuitous, wearisomely verbose explanations rather than providing only the essentials? We free up mental space when we practice a limpid communication style, when we make our thoughts very quick to download.

Another form of mind-clutter comes from the overload of information—also referred to as cognitive overload—and more particularly, information or knowledge about us. Perhaps never before in any generation are we so overwhelmed with information about the self: whether from self-help or motivational books (including this one), videos, workshops, therapy, advice, mentoring, coaching, performance reviews, confrontations, assessments, subliminal messages, websites and blogs. To excess, this too, can turn into mind clutter. We need to consciously decide to manage self-knowledge, sifting through the sand for the few essential gold nuggets that will contribute to the quality of our life, and discarding everything else.

The same applies to the ever increasing fast pace we maintain. This inevitably has a way of making us become worn out like a threadbare piece of cloth that is tenuously being held by weakened fibers. Deciding to organize our thoughts has the same effect as organizing our physical space: it saves time, frees us of distractions, liberates us, makes us lighter and takes us away from harried thoughts. We can organize our thoughts the same way we organize our to do list: by creating a list of the various areas that we are involved in and carving out time to purposefully think about these areas in multi-faceted ways such as adopting a global perspective, practicing visionary, big picture thinking, focusing on important details, using judgment and wisdom, considering entrepreneurial risk taking aspects, entertaining flexibility or versatility, pondering financial aspects, creating a strategy and mapping out execution, to name a few. This purposeful, strategic thinking prevents irregular thoughts that are characteristic of a harried mind.

It also follows that part of de-junking involves creating personal downtime. When a *New York Times* reporter interviewed several recent winners of McArthur Genius Grants, a striking number said they kept cell phones and iPods off or away when in transit so that they could use the downtime for thinking.[7] Time for renewal is, therefore, essential in clearing mind clutter. Meditation and other forms of quiet contemplation are actually a part of the leadership arsenal.

A concomitant aspect of this renewal is the notion of silence. Just as we can be bogged down from over-doing, over thinking and over processing of new information, so we can also, at times, be derailed by over-speaking. As was aptly expressed by *Inner Space in Covent Garden,* "we need to disconnect from all outside things from time to time because [we are] plugged into this person or that person, and to situations. There are many sockets we have all over the place which constantly give [us] current ... sometimes we have so many of these currents coming into us that we short circuit."[8] In the midst of our daily noise, both internal and external, we benefit immensely when we stop to consciously hear the silence between sounds. What could you have left unsaid yesterday? Last week? What difference would it have made in terms of your current state of mind?

Think of an important meeting or encounter that you were involved in. Now reflect on what impact silence on your part would have had on the situation and on the ensuing mind space that the spoken words appropriated. There is much to be gained indeed in cultivating some silence and we encourage you to schedule quiet recreations for your mind just as you would schedule other forms of recreations. The outer silence will lead to inner silence and will generate a calm stability and the power of self-control as you temporarily quiet some of your mental noise.

Another way to release your mind of inconsequential thoughts and mind clutter is to consider setting some time aside such as just before going to bed at night, and getting into the habit of sitting in a quiet spot, closing your eyes and mentally doing a quick scan of the day's events from the moment you started your day. View the day's events and communications objectively and dispassionately, without emotional vesting in the circumstances, merely as one would watch a documentary of someone else's day. Make a mental note of anything that is important and release the rest by imagining it floating away effortlessly as feathers on the breeze. This is a calming exercise that declutters the mind.

We recommend that you create a plan for purging your mind of unproductive thoughts, that is, for performing a mental catharsis by determining which recurrent thoughts regarding yourself, your leadership and the people surrounding you, are useless and clog your thinking. This will free up precious mental energy and increase your emotional bandwidth. And we then encourage you to decide which areas of your life and your leadership needs more conscious, superior thinking. This will bring an inward calm and a bright tranquility will creep into your being. We predict that it will be a powerful springboard that will take you to enhanced mental and emotional clarity. It will help you realize your full greatness for, as Pascal put it: "Man's greatness lies in his power of thought."

LEADERSHIP EXPLORATIONS

Scrape Off Old Paint: The Power of Your Thoughts

Consider the following aspects of your life and note, where appropriate, three examples of behaviors, worries, or intentions that take energy and are distractions, and that cause guilt or clutter your life. Then decide on the most potent action that you can take to de-junk your life.

Relationships

Old Paint	Most Potent Action

- Is there someone you need to forgive?
- Do you invest your time and energy in your most important relationships?
- Which of your relationships are unhealthy?

Finances

Old Paint	Most Potent Action

- Do you live within your means?
- Are you accumulating wealth?
- Do you manage your debt?

Health

Old Paint	Most Potent Action

- Do you treat your body with kindness?
- Do you feed your mind with progressive thoughts that honor you and others?
- Are you currently walking on your spiritual path?

Habits

Old Paint	Most Potent Action

- Which habits waste your time?
- Which habits cause you to feel guilty?
- Which habits prevent you from moving ahead?

Environment

Old Paint	Most Potent Action

- What parts of your home environment are uncomfortable or a source of irritation?
- What parts of your physical work environment hamper your productivity?
- Do you lack a "Third Place"? (Your first place is your home; your second place is your workplace).

INTERVIEW

Scrape Off Old Paint: The Power of Your Thoughts

Scott Duncan
President & Chief Executive Officer, DORMA Architectural Hardware

I confess that I have not been a model of balance between work, family and other pursuits. I know that I only have 24 hours in a day. I find myself parsing out time in 5 or 10 minute blocks.

From a business perspective, I have an approach that seems to work well for applying limited resources to unlimited opportunities. When I arrived at my current company, there was a well-held belief that we had very limited opportunities, and we were almost doomed to fail because we were 1/20th the size of our competitors. The company was scrambling to compete, David vs. Goliath. And we were David. The previous leaders were all trying to act "like Goliath" and had failed.

- *We looked at our market position and our SWOT. We recognized that competing with the market leaders was like the colonial army going 'muzzle to muzzle'. We needed to be different and find our own niche.*
- *We created a short list of five strategic objectives with a few sub sets: Profitable Growth; Strengthen Our People; Enable Market-Driven Growth; Drive Process Excellence; Strengthen Our Financial Position. If anyone was working on something that was not directly connected to these strategic objectives, they were asked to challenge their investment in that task. We set priorities and put several projects on indefinite hold.*
- *Personal goals were created to support the strategic objectives. These goals were aligned with incentives. Each person on the leadership team presented their goals to the group and "connected the dots" to show how we were all aligned. We paid for performance on those goals. This was our BIG BLUE ARROW exercise. We are aligned! Monthly meetings provide a forum for reviewing the team goals and achievements.*

- *Company P&L's are shared with all employees monthly to communicate the impact of improvements, scrap, sales, etc. on the bottom line. We connect the dots with all employees between the cost of benefits, raw material and our ability to make a reasonable profit.*

  So, the simple answer is that if you are sure of what you must accomplish and why, it is easier to sort through the maze of opportunities. Today, we understand that we have more opportunities than we can fund. We sort the opportunities using a simple 'impact vs. cost/risk/ time' approach. Our internal battle cry is: "Where we focus, we win."

CHAPTER ELEVEN

Stand Up Straight
The Power of Courage

"Courage can't see around corners, but goes around them anyway."

MIGNON MCLAUGHLIN

Fear is the constant companion of the leader. To lead is to act in spite of this fear. Your fears will change over the course of your career but they will stalk you relentlessly. Early fears of embarrassment will turn to fears of failure. Your challenge is to act in the face of these fears. There cannot be genuine power without courage–the courage to act. This part of your leadership portrait is not a pastel job. We encourage you to have thoughts like vibrantly colored paint. Sit back for a few moments and think about past events in your leadership journey where you opted not to seize an opportunity because of fear. How does this feel now? Seeing it from today's perspective, were your fears justified? Now switch tapes and play a different movie: see yourself seizing that very same opportunity with your consciousness today. How are you doing? Is the fear diminished? Is it even there? How often have we had fears in the past that we have overcome? Think of the first time you rode a bike or the first time you spoke in public.

We encourage you to step up to your own greatness, every day, at every opportunity that presents itself. This requires courage—the courage to believe in your own personal power, in your ability to express your greatness in the moment, to be receptive to any possibilities that come your way despite any inner fears. "Courage," as Arthur Koestler put it, "is never to let your actions be influenced by your fears."

Here is a paradox: Fear is an emotional asset, if we see it as a messenger of important information. It tells us that what we are afraid of must be challenging and risky for us; if not, we would not fear it. And power comes from having the courage to face those challenges and risks and making a commitment to not let the fear stand in the way of achievement, in the way of reaching our highest potentiality. If we befriend fear, it becomes adrenaline for the soul. It gives us the energy and the exhilaration of action, it gives us courage. And courage, once committed to, carries power. In fact, courage, supplemented by self-confidence, becomes a formidable source of power. It's common to believe that being courageous is synonymous with having no fears, while the opposite is true: having courage is acting despite our fears. It is going after precisely that which we are afraid to do. As Eleanor Roosevelt put it, courage is "looking fear in the face."

It's worth noting that fear is a companion of all leaders. It does not vanish in the senior leadership ranks. Rather, fears mutate in accordance with the increasing personal challenges that come with the territory and the more practice leaders get in taming their fears, the more courageous they become. Seasoned leaders use fear to their advantage—that is, they let it fuel their courage. They feel the fear but stay, nonetheless, steadfast to their purpose; they have developed a stoutness of mind and the professional will to forge right ahead at steady speed toward the achievement of their goals, relegating fear to the back seat. Patton said: "Courage is fear holding on a minute longer." Are there issues right now in your life where, no matter how challenging or discouraging they are, holding on longer would make a difference? How might a courageous outlook fortify your resilience and expand your repertoire of coping mechanisms?

What exactly is courage in a leader? It is that quality of mind or spirit that enables you to face change, risk and the unknown with self-possession, confidence and resolution. It suggests an inner strength on which you can draw when in difficult and challenging times. It is synonymous with mettle, which the dictionary defines as that capacity to rise to the challenge. It is resolution to pursue your purpose against all odds. Courage is doing the unpopular when you know it is the right thing to do. It is being petrified with fear but acting anyway. What is your personal definition of courage? If you practiced courage every day, at every opportunity, at every meeting, in every conversation, in all your internal dialogue, what would this be like? What image of you emerges? What would happen if you intentionally made several courageous decisions next week? What would happen to your stature as a leader?

There is an element of exhilarating energy when we choose to practice courage. It gives us vitality and vigor. It pushes us, propels us forward. It gives us permission to use all of our talents and it sometimes even surprises us with a showing of talents and strengths that we were unaware we possessed. Acting courageously opens up an unexplored storage of personal gifts. Which unopened gifts do you think you might find in your repertoire, if you act with unbridled courage?

How does one develop courage? Some of us are predisposed to have a high degree of courage which comes naturally. Others have to make an intentional effort to practice courage: committing to it, determining to flex their courage muscle. So how do we strengthen that muscle? At a minimum, courage entails the ability to let go of certainty, to be able to slide in and out of the boundaries of certitude and face ambiguity and chance, as real possibilities when taking risks. When we are courageous, we intentionally develop a mind-set of expecting possible deviation and the inability to be deterministic, trusting that our judgment and intuition will help us deal with whatever surfaces in the moment. That is the emblem of the confident leader who, after having done the required due diligence, is able to live with incertitude.

Conventional thinking decrees that courage is developed one measure at a time, going from small doses to increasingly larger ones.

There may be times, however, that call for an audacious move, requiring large doses of courage. When the opportunity calls, answer it. Take that giant, courageous step, make the bold move that is in line with what you want to achieve for those you lead. Do it, trusting that, in the doing, the courage manifests itself and carries you through. Courage is an emotional muscle—the more you practice it, the stronger it becomes.

Leadership is difficult work and no matter how you show up, there will likely be those who will criticize you. We develop courage when we free ourselves from the shackles of the opinion of others. Doing otherwise is a sure way to erode some of your power to act. Dare to be yourself, to take the opposite direction, if need be: to express what you know is right, to go against conventional opinion. It's venturing out into the rough seas and trusting that you will generate the courage to ride the wave of criticism. To be courageous, one also needs to be comfortable with failure and to develop the resilience of going from one setback to another, without losing that initial passion, and retaining the will to begin again and again.

We enhance our ability to act courageously by thinking innovatively about ourselves—using a new framework for viewing ourselves, a framework of possibility, of being wide open to what we could be capable of undertaking, using an audacity of imagination, stretching ourselves to the full limit of what we think we are capable of and then pushing one step further until we are at our very edge. Imagine yourself there. How much courage do you need to get there?

What do you see yourself accomplishing? What is the first step you can take toward this? What do you have to do to reprogram yourself so that you own this vision of yourself? Is the vision totally transparent to you? If not, what is missing? How can you clarify it further? What are potential roadblocks? How many of these are created by you? We encourage you to use a highly inquisitive and analytical approach on yourself as you paint the courage part of your portrait. For example, what are your deepest vulnerabilities, the ones you might talk about only to your most trusted friend, late at night? Despite them, we encourage you to step out of your circle of comfort and do it anyway.

Finally, the most effective process for developing courage is to cast a glance backward and forward in your life's journey. Look back over past events and memories and search for the gifts that you would never enjoy today if you had not acted with courage. Now direct your gaze to the future and determine the three major targets that you want to achieve. What are the major fears associated with these desired achievements, the fears that require the topmost courage on your part? Now think of one action—the most courageous one—that you can take today for each of these targets. This is putting your courage in motion.

There will be times when events or circumstances call for courage greater than we possess. As well, different circumstances require a different measure of courage. Delivering a presentation to a 500-person audience requires a different brand of courage than delivering the same presentation on national TV. Courage is expandable. So is your ability to avail yourself of just the right amount of courage that you need, trusting your capacity to do so.

Powerful leaders take bold, surefooted steps. Are you tiptoeing through your leadership? Courage is about your personal evolution—taking yourself from your shadow to your light, to the point where you are totally in your power, at ease with who you are and confident that you have the fortitude to do whatever it takes to lead yourself. It's about shaping yourself. For powerful leaders, courage is a way of life, a habit. Make it a lifelong habit to dip into your palette daily for courage.

LEADERSHIP EXPLORATIONS

Stand Up Straight: The Power of Courage

List below five courageous leaders in history:

1. _____
2. _____
3. _____
4. _____
5. _____

Nominate five leaders that you personally have known, at any organizational level, and that you consider courageous:

1. _____
2. _____
3. _____
4. _____
5. _____

For each leader that you identified above, note the ways in which you are most like them in terms of courage.

Review the list of fears below and circle your top three:

Going over budget on a project

Making a presentation to the Board

Dealing with an irate customer

Firing a low performing employee

Having a difficult conversation with a direct report or other stakeholder

Managing a toxic boss

Coping with a difficult colleague

Managing with a reduced or limited budget

Making an announcement to various stakeholders about impending changes that will adversely impact others

Dealing with a complex issue
Introducing new technology
Not having enough time for family
Not having enough time for self
Motivating others
Missing an important deadline
Not having the necessary answers at crucial times
Not meeting sales quota
Producing revenues well below budget

For each of your top three fears, think of an example of when you demonstrated courage in a leadership role.

Fear #1: _____
Example: _____
_____
_____
_____
_____
_____

Fear #2: _____
Example: _____
_____
_____
_____
_____
_____

Fear #3: _____
Example: _____
_____
_____
_____
_____

INTERVIEW

Stand Up Straight: The Power of Courage

Jeffrey C. Hawkins
Executive Director, Algonquin Child and Family Services

Courage is an interesting concept as it can be as much about doing something as doing nothing. The latter piece for me has been about having the courage to give up control to others versus impacting a situation directly, in other words, learning to lead through others. It's about being comfortable in letting go. In theory, it may seem like an easy concept, but when you see people in the team articulating thoughts and going in directions that you are not entirely comfortable with, it is easy to forget and step in. And when those same people turn to me on difficult decisions, it takes some resolve to put it back on them by assuming the role of coach.

As leaders, we all have situations where we did not opt to act courageously. I can think of one situation, in particular, where I did not step up to the plate and display courage. A key manager developed a chronic health condition that took him away from work for some time before he was medically cleared to do the job again. I had a personal relationship with him and his family outside of the workplace and I knew that he needed the income.

The reality is that he had neither the resolve nor the stamina and mental agility to continue to do the job. Despite clear indications and feedback from the team that this was the case, I rationalized that he would get back on his feet and decided not to do anything about it. Eventually his health forced him into long term disability and he left the organization. With a new hire, it became clear just how much the organization had been impacted by my avoiding the issue.

In hindsight, I know that I was not fair to the organization, the team and the colleague with the health issue for that matter. What I learned from this is that, as a leader, you need to observe the boundaries between your role and personal relationships. No matter how strong the friendships, there has to be that fine, invisible line between your professional role as a leader and your personal affiliations. You need to have the courage to set aside personal considerations and make clear and fair decisions that are driven by the imperatives of the business. It's what you owe to the organization, the other team members and your customers—it's what you are charged with, as a leader.

If I were to give an example of a situation where I exercised great courage, it is through re-structuring. In my role as the senior executive of a public sector agency, I have seen a three fold plus increase in the past six years in the size of the agency, financially, with personnel and geographic catchments. Increasing the leadership capacity has become a necessity. This is the opportunity. At the same time individuals within the senior management structure appeared to have reached their capacity of skill to effectively perform their portfolios. These are individuals who have been extremely loyal to the organization and me personally through a difficult merger process and hung in there with ever expanding portfolios. Although the need for organizational redesign and capacity increase was openly recognized, the senior managers assumed that the issue would be solved by increasing the number of people who supported them and did not recognize that we needed to fill those positions with individuals who were more developed to assume new executive roles. I was facing a difficult and sensitive people issue.

I made it clear that there was a need for organizational redesign and engaged two chief executive officer colleagues that are respected in the field to work with me as consultants to provide an outside lens, analyze and make recommendations on what was needed. I indicated to the senior management team that this was the strategy I was going to adopt and that the recommendations would be shared, but that I would make the final recommendations to the board of directors. At the same time, it was important that I continue to engage the senior folks in the process by maintaining full transparency as we went along with strategies such as sharing with them a draft of the terms of reference for the chief executive officer consultants and asking for everyone's input, having the consultants meet the senior staff collectively and individually, doing a collective exit interview on their time in the organization and having them present their final recommendations to the group rather than to me personally. The distinction in all this was that participation was for input and not shared decision making in the recommendations. It required courage on my part to continue to maintain this position, despite some of the unhappiness of those involved.

I chose to meet with each senior manager prior to the final report being shared to indicate that it would be transformational in nature, and that I would need their assistance to move it forward. It was very difficult for me not to sugar coat or rescue them on what they would hear, but to sit back and let them hear unconditionally from the consultants. The final recommendations are certainly transformational and impact all the current senior roles by putting another director level in place consisting of three positions between myself and the roles of these folks. It also defines the roles in a manner such that the incumbent senior managers do not have the core competencies for the next level of leadership.

I am being consistently tested to do less dramatic changes that are more transitional or incremental, but I have maintained my courage to stand firm by the adopted recommendations and to pursue this strategy that I know, without a doubt, to be the right one. The lesson I learned here about courage is: once you have done all your due diligence, you need to move forward and not waver.

CHAPTER TWELVE

Your Ultimate Advantage

The Power of Focus

"The successful man is the average man, focused."

SOURCE UNKNOWN

It has been said that if everything is important, nothing is important. As a leader, what are the two or three things that are most important to you? What are your passions? What legacy do you wish to leave? What single work of art do you want to paint? Do these things get the greater part of your energy, time, and attention? If not, then you are on the road to mediocrity as a leader. That single-purpose focus is the source of formidable leadership power. At its purest level, it is what Martina Navratilova means when she says: "I try to concentrate on concentrating." It is a dedicated, disciplined, and targeted focus of attention.

Successful leaders are very adept at practicing this laser-like focus of attention. Bill Gates declared once that part of his success is certainly due to the fact that he focuses in on a few things. These words are echoed by Eric Schmidt of Google who said: "I keep things focused. The speech I give every day is: *"This is what we do. Is what we are doing consistent with that, and can it change the world?"* [9]

To achieve that power of focus, you need to first have a high degree of clarity about what truly matters to you. Over the years, we accumulate beliefs, practices, habits and other intellectual and emotional burdens that no longer serve us. (See Chapter 10.) We need to recognize these, honor them and shed them. It's akin to periodically purging your Inbox from unneeded items and emptying your trash folder. Imagine the sense of renewal and freedom of focus that you would have if you periodically and consistently performed this form of mental housekeeping–if you ruthlessly budgeted your attention to allocate it on only what matters.

You need to be ruthless about what you decide to concentrate on, setting aside anything and everything that does not contribute to the achievement of your goals. This is leadership on steroids: Having total clarity about what are the crucial elements of leadership and then deciding to be intentional about where you choose to direct your attention, in the process developing a specialized mental vision which will allow you to emotionally and intellectually see just what you need to see in order to achieve your purpose. Just like birds have excellent binocular vision for judging distances, so you develop an ability to focus on only what will help you to go the distance. This means not wasting energy reliving the past and staying in the present and future. Take an inspiration from Marie Curie who stated: "I never see what has been done; I only see what remains to be done."

What you focus on grows. What do you want to grow? What are two or three areas that, if you decided to bring into focus, would make a significant difference in your power to lead? Are there any important relationships that you need to bring into sharper focus in your leadership journey? Do the people who support you occupy a focal point? What about those who challenge you? What might you gain from focusing some of your attention on them? What would happen if you took a step back and focused on the bigger picture of your life? What do you see? Is it where you want to go?

Just as you gain power by what you focus your attention on, so you dissipate your power by not being aware of your habits. What habits form you? Examine these carefully: are any of these diluting your power on a consistent basis? What would change in your life if you resolved right now to start each day by asking yourself and responding to these two questions: What are the most important things I need to focus all of my attention on today to be successful? What can I do today to bring me closer to getting the results I want in these important areas? Then imagine yourself zooming in on those areas and directing all of your focus toward getting the results you want.

What might you accomplish at the end of one year? Understanding your focusing habits will allow you to determine what you need to compensate for and will pay dividends. For example, if you have a habit of being detail-oriented, you may fall prey to the greatest prodigality, wasting an inordinate amount of precious time painstakingly focusing on data at the expense of the wider, long-range ramifications. That automatic focus of attention may prevent you from seeing all the possibilities in front of you and therefore, may erode your power.

Take charge of your focus and resolve to develop your time leadership competence by being on the alert about your habitual inclinations—and that includes intrusive, unwanted thoughts. You may, at times, find yourself in a situation where you don't have total control over the complexity and forces that govern your particular context. There is one aspect, however, that you always have total control over and that is your thoughts, being particularly aware how thoughts drive your emotions and how your emotions can divert your focus and dictate your actions. Being sentient, that is, consciously perceiving and developing your choice-making consciousness, is a powerful advantage indeed.

Your focus of attention determines your results—your entire reality, in fact. It is a powerful mental force at your disposal; so powerful it can even alter the structure of your brain, as outlined by Jeffrey Schwartz, MD and Sharon Begley in their book, *The Mind and the Brain: Neuroplasticity and the Power of Mental Force*.[10] Individuals can learn to change how their brain responds to circumstances by intentionally focusing their attention in a different direction. Think of what this self-directed neuroplasticity can do for you. And the more you practice focusing, the more you increase your ability to stay focused. It's like exercising a focusing muscle.

We encourage you to be on the alert for recurrent, intrusive thoughts that divert your focus of attention. Resolve to keep purging these from your mental operating system as soon as they surface; be determined to direct your attention toward a central point of focus—totally concentrating on what makes a difference. Being more conscious of your thoughts and in charge of your focus of attention, then, is a crucial step in painting your leadership masterpiece—a portrait of you, in focus, at your most potent self—mentally and emotionally. What dent will you put in your own universe?

LEADERSHIP EXPLORATIONS
Your Ultimate Advantage: The Power of Focus

What values are most important to your organization?

1. _____
2. _____
3. _____
4. _____
5. _____

What leadership principles are most important to you?

1. _____
2. _____
3. _____
4. _____
5. _____

What is the most exciting future for your organization that you can imagine?

_____
_____
_____
_____
_____
_____
_____
_____
_____
_____
_____
_____
_____
_____
_____

Reflecting on what you wrote in these sections, how will these statements impact where you will focus your attention in your leadership, i.e., what are your leadership themes (e.g., innovation, personal accountability, teamwork)? Please write your three core leadership themes below.

_____

_____

_____

_____

_____

INTERVIEW

Your Ultimate Advantage: The Power of Focus

Mark Ahrens–Townsend
Executive Vice President, Business Development
LibreStream Technologies Inc.

We all read them—the great books of business like Crossing the Chasm, Good to Great *and* Profit from the Core*—books that tell us the importance of focus, the importance of deciding what our businesses are and probably more importantly what they are not. But as clear and sensible as these books seem, the discipline of focus is not an easy or often chosen path. Focus seems counterintuitive to risk reduction through diversification, but in actual fact most great businesses focus on one (or maybe two) areas and the path of 'reduced' risk is the one where we put all of our eggs in one basket and become the best at one thing.*

When I took over as President & Chief Executive Officer of Infocorp, a $6M in revenue publicly traded software company in 1997, I took over the job of reshaping and focusing a company which over its ten-year history had pursued many business opportunities in a number of different markets, on five continents. The company's originating founders did not have a united view of where to focus the business, and as a result, the company was in disarray with large financial losses and depleted financial strength. On my first day, I had to stand up in front of 300 irate shareholders at our annual general meeting and explain my plan to fix the company's many problems and challenges while at the same time pursue opportunities we believed the company could successfully capture.

Long before reading Good to Great, *I had to decide first things first, i.e., who was on the bus and who was off. Looking back it was the first stage of focus. My uncle, who had been a well respected senior executive with MacMillan Bloedel, gave me this advice: that I would only be successful if I surrounded myself with top notch people. I knew that was true and there was plenty of great talent in the company who had stuck through some very tough times to form a go-forward nucleus. But some of the very good ones had different views of where the company should go, even though I had included them in the process of analyzing the brutal facts and coming up with a new strategic plan. When they announced they could not support the new direction and focus, I made no attempt to keep them and let them walk out the door. Having great people with passion on the team is key, but they have to share your vision and focus and discipline or else they must leave to pursue other avenues.*

What happened next was amazing—a relatively inexperienced but knowledgeable and highly supportive and motivated management team formed around a disciplined strategy to focus on the strengths and top opportunity of the company. In my first week, tough decisions were acted upon—our Toronto staff was let go, the New York office was closed, and our Florida operation reduced in size by two-thirds. Within three or four months, our European subsidiary and the remainder of the Florida office were also closed. We focused on our business, cut any non-core expense and lived by collecting our swollen accounts receivable left over for us from the prior leadership. We skirted dangerously close to bankruptcy on several occasions, but somehow all of a sudden the business was easier to understand, easier to explain and much easier to manage. Things that used to be complex, and visited repeatedly, were now simpler to understand and decide upon. Sales started climbing, expenses dropped, productivity improved, morale jumped immensely, margins climbed, and within five months, the company was turned around, from a hemorrhaging financial mess to delivering its all time best quarterly financial performance with a bottom line pure profit (i.e. no capitalization tricks) of over 20 percent of revenue.

What I learned from this experience was the power of focus. What I also learned is that focus was a key driver in uniting people to a common vision and, as I described in the Infocorp situation, the results were amazing and exhilarating. I also learned that being able to lead through focus, and by example, was a powerful set of skills to bring into turnaround situations. Less than two years later, I was thrust into the position of President & Chief Executive Officer of Norsat International. Norsat had its own unique set of challenges and, again, I was in charge of a company in dire financial straits, but this time, I had already seen how things can change quickly through hard work and a disciplined and focused team of very good people. It's like a recipe—you add the ingredients, follow the steps and, at least for my experience, achieve a predictable and successful result.

So on the topic of focus, this is what I have learned:

1. Focus needs to be based on something—what is it that you and your company are going to be the best at?

2. Deciding on a vision, a strategy and the focus of a business requires a strong team—choose your people carefully. (I personally like to interview people a minimum of three times, all in different situations at different times of the day, with the last interview diagramming out my business on a white board, explaining its strengths and opportunities, challenges, and threats and seeing what the person that I am interviewing can contribute to the discussion.) Look for smart and capable people, but look harder for people with high EQ who can work well in a team.

3. Resist strongly the temptation to de-focus … many strategic plans are based on the next phone call. Don't do it. Look for opportunities but be prepared to turn many away and celebrate it when you do.

4. After you find the right people, empower them—give them not only a business plan and a vision to focus on, but also a set of principles which they can use in an empowered way to make decisions that are good for all of your key stakeholders. The speed of the business can accelerate so much with this simple step.

5. Set goals, measure them and celebrate their achievement—this is a simple step, but it is very important to know where you are.

6. Delegate—if you've chosen really good people, then let them grow and take on more for you and the organization. Good people respond really well to this and feel empowered.

7. Communicate clearly, openly and often—at both Infocorp and Norsat this was so important for buy-in, for observation and for clear understanding between people and departments. This applies to stakeholders inside and outside of the company.

8. When a person on the team isn't a part of the team—move fast and let them go. I anguished hard over many of these decisions and, without fail, after having terminated their employment with the company, I felt I should have moved more quickly.

9. *And finally, a good friend of mine and a founder of Infocorp had an expression that I have used many times since I first heard it, and then later understood it. He used to say: "If you want to see what's in the lemon, squeeze it." The point of this phrase is that many people look and act professionally when there is no pressure. The times when you see what they are really made of is during difficult and challenging circumstances. It's a great way to assess people and a great adage to remind yourself of your own performance in difficult and trying times.*

CHAPTER THIRTEEN

Bob, Weave, and Keep Moving

The Power of Resilience

"A great sculpture can roll down a hill without breaking."

MICHELANGELO

All leaders, at some point in their career, have to cope with extreme changes. Markets decline. Projects overrun. People quit. Products fail. Teams fight. Are you tough enough to prevail? Do you have leadership resilience? Vincent Thomas Lombardi, one of the most successful coaches in the history of American football, talked about mental toughness as "spartanism." Spartanism, like the ancient Greek people from whom its name derives, encompasses many admired qualities–among them rigorous self-discipline and courage in the face of adversity or danger. This type of mental toughness is the essence of resilience, the ability to cope successfully with setbacks, and to bounce back. It's the coveted capacity to recover from drastic change and to adjust easily and rapidly to whatever hand one is dealt. When we look at the leadership environment today, it is not only desirable, but in fact, imperative for a leader to foster a high

131

degree of resilience. You need to be able to manage your own reaction to adversity before you can manage ever increasingly complex and chaotic situations involving other people. As a leader, resilience should be a prime tool in your emergency preparedness kit. It's the "black box" of power.[11]

Where does one start in developing resilience, in fostering a tough mental attitude? There is no doubt that resilience is primarily an inside job. One major component of resilience is the ability to use self-discipline and to control one's impulses. There is a well known study which was conducted by Stanford University's Michael Mischel which involved four-year-olds and marshmallows. The researcher wanted to study impulse control in four-year-olds so he set out to conduct the following experiment. He placed a group of four-year-olds, one at a time, in a room and placed a marshmallow in front of them. He told the children that they could eat the marshmallow right away, but if they waited for a few minutes until he returned from going out to finish an errand, when he came back, if they had not eaten the marshmallow, they would receive a second marshmallow. What ensued was interesting: One third of the children ate the marshmallow right away. Another third tried to control their impulse but eventually gave in and ate their treat. But another third of the children, even though they were tempted, were determined to wait for the second marshmallow and did not eat the one in front of them. The researchers followed these children at age 18 and some interesting findings were reported. The children who had no impulse control were more likely to overreact to frustration, to be overwhelmed by stress, to have a sharp temper and to give up when faced with failure—all signs of low resilience. While the children who showed impulse control displayed the opposite: they handled frustrations well, they performed well under pressure, they had self-reliance, were able to concentrate better and followed through on plans—all hallmarks of resilient individuals.

Seeing the correlation between impulse control and resilience, are you able to delay short-term gratification for a longer term goal? What areas of your life are being gratified at the expense of more worthwhile longer term benefits? What do you need to stop doing now that is preventing you from achieving these longer terms goals?

This impulse control, this self-discipline, manifests itself also in task tenacity. It's about staying with something that we perceive as valuable to us and seeing it to completion—it's about not letting setbacks, derailments, temporary constraints, the naysayer, and other noise get in the way of accomplishing anything of value that we set out to do.

Equally important, resilience means quickly dropping what turns out to be worthless. Resolve to let go of any aspects that lose their positivism, aspects that no longer serve you well or may no longer be available to you and have the determination to find new ways. We encourage you to actively cultivate a mindset of detachment, reframing how you view a loss, for example, from seeing it as something that you are suddenly deprived of, to something that has opened up a space for different aspects of equal, and often, greater value. This mindset will propel you to replace feeling sorry for yourself to proactively generating new ideas and possibilities.

The self-discipline of resilience also requires a well honed ability to manage one's thoughts, feelings, and actions and an understanding of how the three are interrelated. Knowing the impact that your thoughts can have on your emotions, resilient individuals catch themselves when non-productive thoughts enter their consciousness and reroute their thinking to what serves them. They also understand the disruptive effect that their feelings could have on their behavior and act as emotional sentinels, actively working on intercepting negative, self-defeating feelings and emotions. This is not about sublimating these feelings and emotions, but rather about being aware of them, facing them head on, acknowledging them for what they are—useless and counterproductive—and quickly moving on. An individual who practices this type of self-awareness is at the high noon of self-management—a very advantageous spot to be indeed.

The real battle for resilience is inside your head: think about your own difficult emotions, for example—you can turn them to your advantage. Take fear, for example. Can you convert it into anger, which in turn can take you out of the inertia caused by fear? How about shame? Can you turn it into a sense of duty and responsibility, a determination to do better next time? Sadness? Can you turn it into self-empathy? Guilt? Can you stare it square in the face and determine if it is rational? If so, can you deal with the causes, make whatever amends you can and move on? If it is irrational, how about simply resolving to discard it? Regret? Can you examine this consuming emotion and extract valuable life lessons from it that you can actually use and discard the feeling itself as the residual husk once the kernel has been salvaged?

Resilient individuals also use humor as a tool to reduce tension that would otherwise derail them from their purpose. They openly confront others when issues arise and express their feelings freely and authentically but they often do so without an edge in their tone and choice of words. This calm confrontation acts as release which frees up their minds instead of carrying these unexpressed thoughts with them. They are also adept at using silence as a centering strategy. Cultivating these abilities pays dividends.

Because they are so adept at using many of these tools, resilient individuals can solve problems in many different life areas, whether professional or personal, whether comfortable with their surroundings or not. Perhaps above all, they use an existential approach to life, believing that they are uniquely responsible for their own actions and accept the consequences of whatever they undertake. Predominantly independent, they also know when to ask for help, if necessary.

When there is a crisis or difficulty, resilient individuals are able to maintain a laser-like focus on only the things that matter. This will help them conserve their mental, emotional and even physical energy which adds to their power to lead, their power to deal with challenging situations. They expect uncertainties and can hold their nerve and be "on" even when they don't feel at their very best. Additionally, the more they practice this behavior, the more they increase their competence to remain unflustered and in control in the face of stressful and chaotic situations.

One can liken the resilient state to elasticity—that is, we can stretch to the limit due to an adversity but still bounce back to where we started. There is energy in this movement that we can tap into to go back to our starting point, and resume where we left off, but stronger because of the adversity, almost as if the emotional stretch and tension works out our emotional muscles to strengthen them. One definition of resilience is, in fact, the ability to regain original state. Research shows that resilient individuals can quickly process the emotional stages known as SARAH: shock, anger and rejection to move to acceptance and seeking help. This is a power advantage that helps us to move away from being stuck and feeling directionless or exhausted in times of leadership crisis.

Where does all of this strength originate from and how can we add its brilliant hue to our palette as part of our leadership power? There is no doubt that some people are inherently more naturally resilient than others. However, resilience is a mental discipline that can be cultivated through sheer will and practice–through a determination to maintain an internal locus of control no matter how chaotic and stressful surrounding events are. It's about drawing upon all of your resources–physical, mental, emotional, spiritual, and intellectual–in the face of difficulty. Internally, it emanates from a healthy pride in oneself, from self-respect and a strong conviction that whatever happens to us, whether positive or negative, is something that springs from inside.

Taking a helicopter view of your personal and professional life is a valuable exercise in creating a plan for resilience. We function as a system with interdependent parts–a weakness behind the curtain of our personal life, for example, can have an impact on our performance on the professional stage–like a solid chain whose strength can be weakened by one weak link. Often, the weakness develops over time, slowly and in imperceptible ways until the connection breaks and we are left stranded at a time when we need the most resilience. Examine your entire life, every nook and cranny, every component. What do you see? What dented or rusted links do you spot in your life chain? What can you do about strengthening these? Viewing yourself as a system gives you the power of 20/20 sight and ensures that you are not blind-sided by events.

Resilience is also increased as we build community and forge strong connections with others, whether family, friends, associates or spiritual or societal institutions. Insularity is a detriment to building resilience. Being a member of a close-knit community provides the support to respond well to adversity.

Resilience is the *coup de grâce* of your masterpiece portrait. It's about being a master of yourself—someone who has acquired a mental fitness par excellence. There is no doubt that resilient individuals think more clearly and that clarity of thought promotes an intuitive ability. A resilient leader, then, is like a good chess player whose strength lies in the intuitive ability to create effective long term strategic plans and who is quickly able to differentiate meaningful moves from meaningless ones; who can see and utilize the infinite possibilities of the mind; who can concentrate, recognize patterns and focus by eliminating distractions to which non-resilient individuals succumb. It's someone who can dig deep into their mental reserves. Being resilient is a good move.

LEADERSHIP EXPLORATIONS

Bob, Weave, and Keep Moving: The Power of Resilience

Every event presents an opportunity for two choices:

1. A draining practice or reaction

2. A resilience-building practice or reaction

For example:

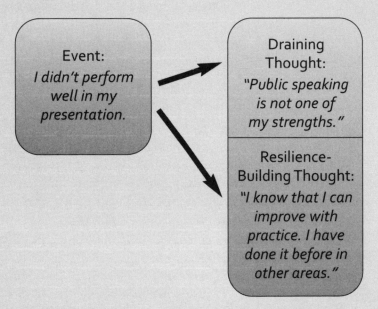

Think about a recent negative event and record a draining thought you might have had and replace it with a resilience-building thought.

| Event: | Draining Thought: |
| | Resilience-Building Thought: |

Explore examples of some things that you need to let go:

_____

_____

_____

_____

_____

_____

Where do you get mired in today's problems as opposed to creating a better tomorrow?

_____

_____

_____

_____

_____

What areas do you tend to take personally that are not personal?

_____

_____

_____

_____

_____

_____

INTERVIEW

Bob, Weave, and Keep Moving: The Power of Resilience

John Sage
Founder, Pura Vida Coffee

Resilience is a topic that has a particular resonance for me because it has a lot to do with the underlying, fundamental challenges I was faced with when I set out to create this company: the challenge of how to fund and finance a growing company that has a social mission. I started by funding the company solely for several years up to 2001. That's when I needed outside capital to continue to support our growth.

The pivotal point was after September 11—trying to raise money then was a daunting task. By early 2002, I had not had much luck. We had created a complex finance vehicle because we are a mix of profit and not-for-profit. So, in the spring of 2002, I had been in Chicago for three days to raise money with zero success. Payroll was due at the end of the month—I had invested $1.5M into the company by that point and I had no other personal resources to invest.

So I left Chicago, empty-handed, for one last meeting—to go to Indianapolis to meet with another possible investor. I was demoralized to say the least. There was a huge snow and ice storm that night, the Interstate highway was shut down on both sides between Chicago and Indianapolis and there was also a big accident with a semi-trailer. I found myself stuck on the highway, not moving, for four hours. It was three days and many months of failure. I called my wife a little after midnight from the car and was weeping from frustration and fatigue. Eventually, the road opened and the cars started moving. I arrived at the hotel in Indianapolis at 4:30 a.m.

I was unable to sleep—you know how that is ... when you are so tired you can't fall asleep. The last thing I wanted to do was to go out and make another presentation for funding. I was to meet a man named Don Palmer. I was so convinced that he would not be interested that the first thing I said to him after shaking his hand is: "Sorry to bother you—you probably won't be interested in this." He said: "Well, you got me out of bed so early; I might as well see what you have ..."

Business is a powerful source of social change—it had always been my fervent desire to bring capitalism and compassion together. I was so certain that he would say, "Hey, this is not for me" that I almost didn't give him an opportunity to respond to what I was saying and I answered for him as I went along. After I had finished the presentation, he said: "Well, this is the most expensive free breakfast I have ever had." He wrote me a check for $30,000 on the spot. I have that check framed and it's hanging in my office. It allowed me to meet payroll. It saved my company. I was starting to regain confidence and know that I was not crazy.

In the following 18 months, I raised $1.8M in the second round. Yes, the markets were down, it was post-9/11, but I persisted and found other people like Don Palmer, who, like me, had this notion that if you bring the rigor of business and money as a social purpose together, it might result in an enormous lever to create social change.

There are about three dozen individuals who contributed to Pura Vida, which is now a company of significantly greater size. I just went to Indianapolis last week to meet with Don Palmer and thank him for his trust.

The stubbornness and resilience helped me cope with the pressure of growing a company and financing it. It helped me stay the course despite formidable odds. I have often been asked what the 'rubber' behind that resilience is—that tenacity I possess. What is it that cushions me? Much of Pura Vida is rooted in strong Christian faith. First of all, it's a company that had its seed planted 20 years ago at the Harvard Christian Fellowship which is where I met my good friend and business partner, Chris. It's a strong partnership that has endured and grown for two decades. Faith provided me the "rubber"—and the catalyst—to pursue and continue my dream.

It came from two sources:

- *I grew up with very strong progressive social activist parents in Berkeley; it was the '60s and my folks were involved in a lot of social causes rooted through faith experience—strong experiences, to seek justice.*

- *My own arduous ten years of keeping the company afloat—it seems that, repeatedly, God's faith sustained me. I would not have been capable of doing it on my own. I believe: "Self-sufficiency is not sufficient."*

Today, I practice an aspect of resilience that is releasing the outcome along with a belief in God's faith. If my pursuit is good, it will continue to prosper. This does not absolve me from my responsibilities to do the work required, but it helps me.

People often try to uncover what qualities make one resilient. But, in my opinion, I wouldn't say that it is qualities that create resilience. For me, it's a part of my wiring and makeup. It's a part of my upbringing. It's a burning desire. For example, I have always tried to answer a question that consumed me for a long time and the question is this: Can you combine two strands that are seemingly opposite?

a. Social justice; an activist-oriented desire—I had been involved in this for a long time. (For example, when I was 11, I was involved in walking precincts for George McGovern. I was involved in boycotts as a kid. I also lived on an Indian reservation in high school.)

b. Enjoying business—as a capitalist.

Traditionally, these two approaches don't blend. You usually pick one, work hard as a capitalist, make money and then give it all away. Certainly that approach can be effective as well. We see a fine example of that in Bill Gates for whom I worked in the past. I wanted to try the other route. I asked myself if business and capitalism that involve risk taking could be used not just for the sake of wealth creation, but also for community transformation.

I am reminded of a quote by Martin Luther King which has always inspired me:

> *"The strong man holds in a living blend strongly marked opposites. The idealists are usually not realistic, and the realists are not usually idealistic ... Seldom are the humble self-assertive, or the self-assertive humble. But life at its best is a creative synthesis of opposites in fruitful harmony."*

The force of power is in combining opposite ideas. The true power is in bringing together opposites. This has been a guiding principle for me.

The melding of two opposites is reflected in a beautiful biblical quotation where Jesus told his disciples to be as wise as a serpent and gentle as a dove. Martin Luther King built this into his sermons: "We must combine the toughness of the serpent and the softness of the dove, a tough mind and a tender heart." To me, that's power.

So the intersection of business and good for the community transferred further leads us to the conclusion that there is a great deal of power in combining these opposites. When you find the intersection between what you enjoy, what you are good at, and what the world needs—that's a wonderful feeling. Then work is more of a source of energy than a drain on your resilience.

CHAPTER FOURTEEN

The Grass Is Indeed Greener

The Power of Optimism

"Pessimism leads to weakness. Optimism leads to power."

WILLIAM JAMES

Leaders are purveyors of hope. They paint a picture of a tomorrow that is better than today. Hope is one of the most powerful elements of leadership. As Luthans and Avolio assert: "The force multiplier throughout history has often been attributed to the leader's ability to generate hope. Optimism is the lifeblood of leadership."[12]

"Even if I knew that tomorrow the world would go to pieces, I would still plant my apple tree." These inspirational words by Martin Luther King epitomize what optimism stands for—a positive life view, an unwavering belief that all is going to turn out well in the end. Optimism is non-negotiable in your quest for leadership power. Just as an optimistic leader can fuel and inspire others to achieve, so it is for yourself: optimism is that precious combustible substance that provides our mental and emotional energy, that which converts our hopes and aspirations into kinetic energy and that allows us to glimpse the realization of our ideas in brilliant Technicolor.

145

Optimism drives us to action. It sets a tone of hope, vitality, and inspiration for others and for you.

When you have an optimistic outlook about your ability to succeed, no matter what goes on around you, you end up at a vantage point. It's like getting the best seat in the house from which you can view yourself executing your desired outcomes. It's watching yourself in your own inspiring movie—with you as the screen writer. That optimistic image of yourself in your mind's eye is more powerful than any other strategy for developing and acquiring personal leadership power. One of the hallmarks of optimistic individuals is that they approach their envisioned plans for themselves and those they lead with a subconscious attitude of "Why not?" Contrast the energy contained in this question with its counterpart, "Why?" They have an abiding belief that they can accomplish what they set out to do. We often spot these people by the potent force of their wills which is unwavering, even in the midst of chaos. Where others might unwillingly take detours, these leaders forge ahead, following the internal directions they set out for themselves.

There is no doubt that optimism gives one a competitive advantage. Where others have resigned themselves to the status quo, leaders with an optimistic outlook seek to take control of their destiny. They believe that they can have a big influence on the future—and that belief fuels their optimism, which in turn fuels leadership power. Powerful leaders are motivated by a strong inner sense of their ability to work with the energy of all situations. They know that they can deal with whatever hand they are dealt, when they put in the effort required. This confidence helps them stay the course, if they deem this beneficial to their desired outcome. As Jeff Bezos, CEO of Amazon, states: "Even once you have a strategy that makes sense and holds together from different angles, optimism is essential when trying to do anything difficult because difficult things often take a long time. That optimism can carry you through the various stages as the long term unfolds."[13] Optimism also enables one to rebound from setbacks faster. In an atmosphere of continuous changes and unpredictability, optimistic leaders stay buoyant. They know that doing otherwise would be self-sabotage.

This takes us to the researcher who probably devoted the most time in studying the traits of optimists, Dr. Martin E. Seligman, former president of the American Psychological Association and Professor of Psychology at the University of Pennsylvania. He has devoted decades to studying optimistic people and reports three traits that they have in common. They view adversity in their lives as temporary as opposed to pessimists who view a negative event in their lives as permanent (unchangeable); they view adversity as specific (not permeating all other aspects of their lives) as opposed to pessimists who view adversity as pervasive (affecting all aspects of their lives); and, finally, they view adversity in their lives as not personal, that is, not entirely their fault, as opposed to pessimists who view adversity as more personal (viewing him or herself as the source of the adversity; that it is all his or her fault). In the face of setbacks or challenges, pessimists are more likely to do worse than predicted and even give up, while optimists will persevere. Optimism, therefore, is a crucial component of personal achievement, and is especially important in times of chaos, change and turbulence. Those who have an optimistic outlook will roll with the punches, will be more proactive and persistent, and will not abandon hope.

John Kennedy put it aptly: "When you have seven percent unemployed, you have ninety-three percent working." This is a particular strength of those who practice optimism—the ability to focus on the potential upside of each situation. Where pessimists see red lights, optimists look for green lights. What red lights are stopping you right now from the full attainment of your leadership power? How many of these might have been installed by you? What is one situation in your life that would change radically if you made a deliberate effort to view it with fresh eyes? How can you reframe what you see in order to glean the upside? What if you took a fearless perspective? How many new doors would you be able to open? Just as optimistic leaders set the tone for others in their organizations, so they also set it for themselves.

One obstacle in our quest for developing an optimistic outlook is the feeling of regret for what has passed. While most emotions are useful and provide information, regret is not one of them. It's a mental energy thief and mental energy is essential to optimism and personal power. Dwelling in the regret lane is also immobilizing. Above all, regret clouds our perception of the present and the future. Truly optimistic individuals are able to move on and let go, without losing faith in themselves and in their future. It's as though their vision allows them to see around the corner and what they see there, invisible to others, is better than what is. All powerful leaders believe that they can make tomorrow better than today—for themselves and for others. This is at the core of their leadership. And while they expect to receive more, they are not derailed if they receive less. So how do you develop this belief in a better tomorrow and the ability to deal with less than what was desired as situations evolve? We believe that one of the secrets of accomplishing this is being in that blissful and ennobling state of appreciation, experiencing the power of gratitude, of counting one's blessings.

When coaching clients in our leadership development practice, we often ask them to list four or five things that they are grateful for, in the moment. We ask them to begin their day with this ritual of appreciation. What are your blessings? How many can you list right now? How would your life change if you began your day, every day, from that perspective?

So, where does optimism come from? Is it something we are born with or is it learned? For some lucky individuals, being optimistic comes naturally. The good news is that, for those who don't have it naturally, optimism is an attitude that can be learned and practiced. You have a unique power to control your thoughts. This makes you the creator of your inner world. What is your internal dialogue? Are there any patterns that you can detect? Are these patterns increasing your personal power? Do they provide unbounded clarity of mind about your purpose, your desired achievements as a leader? Or are they muddying the process by restricting you, by holding you back? If so, what can you do to substitute these internal maps with more viable ones? Optimism is essential to the full development of personal power—it's the foundation for your courage to take bold acts. We encourage you to place optimism at the center of your palette, to dip your brush in it, often and deeply and, to paint broad brush strokes as you make colorful progress in painting your leadership portrait.

LEADERSHIP EXPLORATIONS

The Grass Is Indeed Greener: The Power of Optimism

Write an essay that describes the best possible outcome of your leadership a year from now.

_____
_____
_____
_____
_____
_____
_____
_____
_____
_____
_____
_____
_____
_____
_____
_____
_____
_____
_____
_____
_____
_____
_____
_____
_____
_____
_____
_____
_____
_____
_____
_____

INTERVIEW

The Grass Is Indeed Greener: The Power of Optimism

Willard (Dub) Hay
Senior Vice President, Starbucks Coffee Company

In reading the passage in the Optimism chapter stating that when you have an optimistic outlook—"it's like getting the best seat in the house from which you can view yourself executing your desired outcomes"—it reminded me of something I learned in my early 20s, and that is, the power of visualization. I used it in flight school when I was preparing to be a naval aviator. Just before a flight, I would find a private spot and sit there and visualize the entire briefing for the flight. I would close my eyes and see everything from starting the aircraft, taxiing onto the runway, to landing. I would visualize formation flying and night flying. When in the air, I would feel I had seen this before. It was very comfortable and familiar to me. Visualization makes things a whole lot easier.

I also use visualization for business when I am going to deliver a speech; I visualize what the audience looks like, who they are. For example, when rolling out our industry leading ethical buying program, I visualize what to say to the farmers or cooperatives—to help them understand what we do and how it would benefit them. I use visualization for any difficult or complicated task. So visualization makes you completely comfortable in a situation where you would normally be uncomfortable. It helps you to imagine a successful outcome.

How do I cope with inevitable adversity? My approach is to get very calm. And how do you do that? Primarily, it comes from experience and learning to trust my instincts. And taking deep breaths ... and looking at what the options are. Not pushing to solutions, but getting into a positive mindset. It's literally choosing that mindset, choosing to be positive. Attitude is a choice. And choosing a positive attitude is a powerful choice. And this comes from a basic understanding that my thoughts affect my feelings and my feelings will affect my behavior.

In addition to adversity, we need to cope with regrets. Some regrets you can't do anything about—a missed opportunity, for example. But if you carry these regrets around with you, they are a negative anchor that prevents you from moving forward and accomplishing the important things. One strategy I have developed is to leave my job at the end of each day with a clean slate and come in fresh the next morning. If you bring work problems home, then you will have problems at home. Resolve to start the day fresh. Ask yourself: "Is my mindset right for what I have to do today?" and "Am I setting a tone that I would want to follow?"

If you are setting an optimistic tone, you will energize yourself and others on your team. I never want to follow someone who is negative. I want to follow someone who inspires me, someone who can paint a big picture.

ENDNOTES

1. Boyd Clarke and Ron Crossland, *The Leader's Voice: How Your Communication Can Inspire Action and Get Results!* (New York: SelectBooks, Inc., 2002), 14.

2. Jean de La Bruyere, French Essayist (1645–1696).

3. John Santrock, *Psychology 7th Edition.* (New York: McGraw-Hill Companies, 2004), 74.

4. James O' Toole, *Creating the Good Life: Applying Aristotle's Wisdom to Find Meaning and Happiness.* (US: Rodale Inc., 2005), 228.

5. Ekhart Tolle, *The Power of Now: A Guide to Spiritual Enlightenment.* (Novato, CA: New World Library & Namaste Publishing, 2004), 18.

6. Leon Festinger, *A Theory of Cognitive Dissonance.* (Palo Alto, CA: Stanford University Press, 1962).

7. Claudia Wallis and Sonja Steptoe, "Help! I've Lost my Focus," *The New York Times Magazine,* 10 January, 2006.

8. *Inner Space in Covent Garden:* Managed by Brahma Kumaris Information Services and Brahma Kumaris World Spiritual University.

9. Tom Spring, "Three Minutes with Google's Eric Schmidt: Google Boss Discusses the Company's Future and Mastering the Art of the Internet Search," *PCWorld.com,* 30 January, 2002.

10. Jeffrey M. Schwartz & Sharon Begley, *The Mind and the Brain: Neuroplasticity and the Power of Mental Force.* (New York: HarperCollins, 2002).

11. Bonnie Bernard and Kathy Marshall, "Exploring the Black Box of Resilience: Unraveling Mysteries," National Resilience Resource Center, College of Continuing Education, Regents of the University of Minnesota.

12. Cited by Martha R. Helland and Bruce E. Winston, *Journal of Leadership & Organizational Studies,* Winter, 2005.

13. Rob Walker, "America's 25 Most Fascinating Entrepreneurs," *Inc.com: The Daily Resource for Entrepreneurs, http://www.inc.com/magazine/20040401/25bezoshtml.*

EPILOGUE

In his widely read book, *Leadership is an Art,* Max DePree declares: "We cannot become what we need to be by remaining what we are." Indeed, when we find in ourselves the power to lead, a new level of energy lifts us out of the tedium of life's routines into the higher calling of leadership.

We encourage you to step up to this calling. Your life, and the lives of the people you lead, will be touched in a way no book can describe. This is the reason that artists paint.

We have committed our professional lives to help leaders enhance their leadership skills. We are passionate about leadership and enjoy sharing our knowledge and experiences with others. As lifelong learners, we welcome the opportunity to hear from you about your leadership journey.

You can reach us at:

greggthompson@bluepointleadership.com

brunamartinuzzi@bluepointleadership.com

INDEX